A GLIMPS

Also by Alan Plowright

Plowright Follows Wainwright
Hot-Foot Through The Highlands

A GLIMPSE OF YORKSHIRE
Alan Plowright

Moorfield Press

First published in Great Britain
by
Moorfield Press 1998

Filmset by
Highlight Type Bureau Ltd, Bradford, West Yorkshire
Printed in England by
The Amadeus Press Ltd, Huddersfield, West Yorkshire

A CIP catalogue record for this book is available from the British Library

ISBN 0 9530 11 92 5

The moral right of the author has been asserted

Cover photograph - near Starbotton, Wharfedale: Alan Plowright
Colour photographs: Alan Plowright

Contents

Acknowledgements

My sincere thanks are due to Harvey Smith, Hannah Hauxwell, Luke Casey and Ian Dewhirst, for allowing me to feature them in this book. I am likewise indebted to the brothers who are featured in the chapter entitled 'The Farm Beside Baildon Moor,' whose names I do not reveal, in order to preserve their privacy.

Acknowledgement is made to John W. Holroyd for the compilation of the maps and sketches.

The following people have kindly allowed the use of illustrations.
J.W. Holroyd – page 17
W. R. Mitchell – pages 18, 81, 126
B. Cockcroft– colour photograph of Hannah Hauxwell
British Waterways – page 48
T. Parker – pages 54, 56, 57
Doncaster Museum and Art Gallery – page 80
I. Dewhirst – pages 94, 95, 98, 99, 101 and colour photograph of himself at Hebden Bridge
Baildon Oral History Group - page 107
H.G.W. Household - page 127
Tyne Tees Television - colour photograph of Luke Casey.

Note for Walkers

Reference is made in this book to certain walks and long-distance footpaths, such as the Dales Way and the Nidderdale Way. The descriptions of these are not intended as definitive guides. If any of the walks mentioned are undertaken, it is advisable to make use of the relevant Ordnance Survey maps and guide books. The use of weatherproof clothing, boots, or sturdy shoes, is also recommended.

Introduction

It is a pleasure to write about Yorkshire, the county that I have lived in for nearly thirty years. When I moved from Nottinghamshire I knew nothing of Yorkshire's wonderfully diverse landscapes and friendly, down to earth people.

My home in Baildon proved convenient for exploration, as a fledgling walker, of nearby Baildon and Ilkley Moors. Since those initial, tentative steps, I have travelled on foot around much of the county, particularly the Dales and North York Moors. Not only have I enjoyed walking the invigorating fells and picturesque valleys, I have followed some of its great arteries, such as the Leeds and Liverpool Canal and the Settle-Carlisle Railway.

The following chapters recount many of the areas that I have become familiar with and they also divulge a little about the lives of people that it has been my privilege to meet.

During my early walks I often passed a farm lying in the shadow of Baildon Moor, which is occupied by two brothers, who moved there sixty-one years ago and have never wished to live elsewhere. Their recollections of life at the farm, which extend to the period prior to the Second World War, are revealed in the chapter entitled 'The Farm Beside Baildon Moor.'

A little farther afield, on the edge of Ilkley Moor, stands Harvey Smith's farm. I have passed it countless times and have wondered of late how Harvey spends his time now that show-jumping does not play such a big part in his life. He was kind enough to enlighten me and readers can find out in 'The Irrepressible Horseman.'

The glare of publicity has receded for that wonderful 'Lady of the Dales,' Hannah Hauxwell, who now lives quietly in her cottage, situated a few miles down the valley from her farm at Low Birk Hatt. Hannah reveals a little about her life and interests in 'Hannah-Nine Years On'.

Everyone who watches Yorkshire Television's *Dales Diary* will be familiar with its originator, Luke Casey, who, through this popular programme, has brought the reality of life in the Yorkshire Dales into our homes. He has travelled the region extensively and interviewed many farmers, craftsmen and other Dalesfolk in beautiful surroundings.

He has a passionate regard for the Dales and its occupants, which is clearly demonstrated in 'The Roving Reporter.'

A man with several appearances on the *Dales Diary* to his credit, is Ian Dewhirst, whose knowledge of Yorkshire and its history is second to none. He spent many years as Reference Librarian at Keighley Public Library, which permitted access to a treasure trove of information that has proved invaluable to his interest in local history. It has also contributed to Ian's outstanding reputation as a public speaker, for he is continually in demand. His upbringing in Keighley and other experiences are outlined in 'Who Said That History Is Dull?'

One person who was unable to assist directly with the compilation of this book, is Henry Jenkins, reputedly Yorkshire and England's oldest man, who died in 1670. However, the memory of this remarkable man, who reached an incredible age, lives on. His fascinating life is revealed in 'That Surprising and Wonderful Man.'

I hope that you will enjoy reading about these people and the featured locations. Perhaps it will promote the discovery of hitherto unvisited places within our exceptional county.

Harvey competing at the Horse of the Year Show 1969.

CHAPTER ONE

The Irrepressible Horseman

I chose the title of this chapter with care, for the majority of people think of Harvey Smith as a show-jumper. This is, of course, quite correct and he is undoubtedly one of the most consistently successful riders in the history of the sport. However, first and foremost, Harvey is a horseman, who was born with a special talent that will never desert him. Horses are his life and even though the adulation and plaudits for his show-jumping exploits have subsided, he is still hard at work with the animals that he loves and respects. In fact, Harvey reckons that he is working harder now than ever before and holidays are merely a pipe dream!

This is how he put it when I visited his home for an informal chat about his life and career. It is a short drive from my home village of Baildon to High Eldwick, where his farm is situated, but it is long enough for me to ponder the kind of reception that awaited me. The V-sign, a reference to his famous gesture at Hickstead in 1971, displayed on his back door, was of no comfort. When I entered, Harvey was snatching a rare break from work to watch the show-jumping that was being televised from, coincidentally, Hickstead. Was this an omen, I wondered? Despite my interruption, he led me, without a word of complaint, to the spacious veranda that occupies pride of place at the front of his house, to ensure that we would not be disturbed.

What a superb vantage point it provides. As we talked I was able to look across the grassy expanse of Baildon Moor to Acre Hill, whose rounded summit presides over a landscape of heath and farmland that slopes gently towards Bingley and the Aire valley. In the eyes of a walker, like myself, it is ideal territory. To Harvey it has the more significant ingredient of being excellent for horses.

He enthuses that the farm occupies an ideal location, the best in Europe, for equine training. Every facility, in his opinion, is available within the compact area between Baildon Moor and Ilkley Moor, whose heather-clad wastes almost reach his back door. Extensive adjacent fields provide the freedom for energetic gallops, whilst the responsive moorland, kind to both horse and rider, facilitates stamina-building canters.

As I listened, I could detect Harvey's no-nonsense Yorkshire honesty and outspokenness, a trait that has often caused conflict with officialdom. I gathered that to him horses are not a means to an end, they need to be nurtured and treated as equals. He believes that horses think on the same level as humans and he always looks at things from the horse's perspective. This does not mean that he becomes over familiar with them, they are initially shown who is the boss and then led along sensibly. In his eyes, a horse that is continually ruffled will become confused and will not perform at its best.

To illustrate this fact, Harvey relates an episode with War Paint, who later became an accomplished show-jumper, but came into his possession with a reputation for waywardness and being foul-tempered. During his first eventful ride, War Paint repeatedly refused to obey instructions and continually reared up, threatening to throw Harvey to the ground. Fed up with this treatment, he whispered into the horse's ear. 'There are two of us here and one of us is gaffer - and that one is me.' By the end of that first session War Paint had decided to do as he was told. He never reared again and proved to be one of the gentlest horses imaginable. Harvey believes that it was not viciousness so much as fear, which caused him to be at odds with everyone, and once his confidence was gained, the battle was won.

Harvey has lived in the locality all his life and has never considered re-locating, for the reasons which I have outlined. He was born and raised in the nearby hamlet of Gilstead, a suburb of Bingley. Contrary to my belief, he was not brought up on a farm. His father owned a building firm and in his teens Harvey worked for him as an apprentice bricklayer, but he admits that he spent more time plumbing and driving diggers and bulldozers than learning the art of laying bricks. Gradually, he took more of an executive position and at the age of twenty-five, became a partner in the firm.

During his schooldays, much of his spare time was spent on a nearby farm and he was put on a Shetland pony at the age of seven by his elder brother, John, who led him around the fields and over Gilstead Moor. Harvey must have been a quick learner, for at the age of eight he entered his first jumping competition, at Bingley Show, in 1947. He rode a pony, Simon, who belonged to Jack Baker, a local farmer. Before his mount could compete, it had to earn its keep by delivering milk, a task that it performed every day of its adult life, until it was killed by lightning in 1963. Harvey jumped with Simon on other occasions, but their outings were limited to a handful each year and were mainly confined to gymkhanas, rather than junior jumping events.

His brother, who was eight years older than Harvey, bred a pony, which he named Amby, after Amby Hainsworth, with whom Harvey spent many hours discussing horses as a young boy. He was a true character, who always had a smile and a cheering word for everyone. Harvey refers to him as the 'Pied Piper of Baildon', who was everybody's friend and a local legend. Amby was particularly popular with children because he let them have full charge of his horse when he was not using it. They would feed and groom it so that it was ready whenever he called at the stable to use it for his next job. He was a 'Jack of all trades,' moving all kinds of cargoes with his horse and cart. In the late nineteen-forties, he was still carrying out furniture removals, despite his considerable age. In his earlier years he was employed as coachman to Sam Walker, of Baildon, who was a very successful businessman in Bradford. Every morning, Amby drove his master down the red shale drive of his home, Pennithorne House, and into Bradford, where Sam Walker had a warehouse, in which he stocked a variety of high-quality worsted and woolen goods, in addition to a wide range of other textiles.

It was at Todmorden Show, in 1953, when he was only fifteen years old, that Harvey decided to give show-jumping a real go. At that time the textile town was part Yorkshire and part Lancashire and he admits to going there as 'green as grass' and watching some of the adult-class jumping competitions. He was not impressed and felt that if he could not get a horse to perform better than those that he had witnessed, it was a 'rum job,' as he told his companion.

Shortly afterwards, at a horse sale in York, Harvey was captivated by a big bay four-year old, which was knocked down in the selling ring for thirty-three guineas. He dashed to a nearby telephone box and rang his father. 'Borrow the money from Lionel' (his companion), was the reply. Fortunately, the new owner was happy to take a small profit and sold the horse to Harvey for forty pounds. He was christened Farmer's Boy and before that month was over, he was at his first show. The rest is history, as they say, for within three years Harvey was jumping for Great Britain on him.

The year that he purchased Farmer's Boy, was Harvey's last at school and even in those early days his defiant streak had surfaced.

A young Harvey at Bingley Show in 1947

He was frequently kept in after the final bell and to redress the balance, Harvey always turned up that much later to school the following morning. He attests that if he had ever joined the armed forces, he would still be doing fatigues! The reality is that Harvey cannot be dictated to, but if someone asks him to do something, he is only too willing to oblige.

During his early years in show-jumping, Harvey was wise enough to make a close study of the established riders. The two that he watched with the keenest eye, were Raimondo d'Inzeo and Pat Smythe. He modelled himself to a great extent on Raimondo, whom he admired for his ability to ride a poor horse and still get a 'very good tune out of it.' Pat Smythe's method, he found, was similar to Raimondo's. Her horses always struck an even rhythm, were always balanced and could jump from any stride.

Harvey's exploits in the show-jumping ring are legendary and are well documented in the several books that he has produced. They are far too numerous to list, but suffice to say that his success was largely due to three important attributes. First and foremost was his unwavering will to win. The others were his toughness and an ability

Harvey near his farm

to take the hard knocks, which the sport demands. Harvey recalls in his books some of the mishaps that he suffered during his career.

At the Bakewell Show, the country's largest of its kind at that time, Farmer's Boy hit a pole in the collecting ring and a wing of the fence flew up, cracking Harvey across the nose and breaking it. He was due in the ring immediately afterwards for the Grades A and B contest and got third place. After half an hour, the bleeding had stopped and he took part in the grand final. After such a knock, that would have deterred weaker riders, he was determined to fight against the odds and it served to improve his performance. Consequently he and Farmer's Boy won the competition.

Later that same month another mishap occurred whilst he was riding the same horse during the Test at the British Timken at Dunston. Halfway through the first round the strap pulled out of his saddle top and he had to free the saddle and let it fall from the horse. Harvey completed the course without incurring any faults and, not wishing to make a fuss, did not try to borrow another saddle. This forced him to jump a further two rounds bareback and he managed fourth place. He had often ridden without a saddle at home and declares that the exercise was not too difficult.

In 1972, shortly before the Grand National, Harvey was invited to ride the Aintree course in a special televised event that was due to take place on the day before the great race. National Hunt jockeys had already tried show-jumping, but now the boot was on the other foot. He relished the challenge, despite nursing three broken ribs, sustained three weeks earlier when a horse had kicked him. On the morning of the ride, Harvey strapped himself up and threw himself around his living room like a yo-yo, much to the amusement of his wife.

Declaring himself fit, off he went to Aintree and all went well until he tried to jump Beechers Brook. His horse, Cashel Fort, jumped to the left and fell, throwing Harvey to the ground. Miraculously, horse and rider were unscathed, so he remounted and completed the course. Since that day Harvey has retained a great respect for National Hunt jockeys, who have to perform such exploits day after day on good and bad horses.

The following day Harvey presented the prize to the Grand National winner, but he was not overawed by the occasion and noticed the acute apprehension shown by the stable lads when they were required to turn their horses loose on the course. They were clearly concerned for the horses' safety and the lad in charge of the winning horse, Well To Do, was so relieved when his charge came back that he burst into tears.

An important factor in breaking into, and making a success of, show-jumping is transport for the horses. This can be very expensive and in his early years in the sport Harvey had to make do and mend, as far as horse wagons were concerned. New ones were too costly, so he and his brother began with a converted Burtons tailors' van and had to do their own maintenance and repairs. Their next vehicle had begun its life as a haulage wagon for ovens and it was also converted to carry horses. Eventually they mastered the art of turning the wagon into a mobile home. On arrival at a show, the horses were boxed and the wagon cleaned out. Then a carpet was laid, a sink unit and Calor gas stove were installed and a bed was put up in the recess above the cab. It was a veritable home from home and just as good as a caravan.

On one unfortunate occasion, just after the birth of Harvey's first son, he journeyed up to Edinburgh for the Royal Highland Show and was naturally anxious to get back home as early as possible. Once

Harvey Smith's farm, High Eldwick

View of Baildon Moor from Harvey's veranda

Horses being exercised on the gallops

The road from Kettlewell to Park Rash and Coverdale

the show was over he pushed the wagon hard on the return journey. All went well for a while until his companion, a young lad called William Halliday, went into the back to make some sandwiches. Then disaster struck. A wheel came off the wagon and it overturned into the middle of the road. There was no sound from the two horses they were carrying as Harvey clambered out of the cab, but as soon as he opened the door at the back they both greeted him with a whinny. They lay on their sides with the gas stove, the pots and pans and William on top of them. He was unhurt and remarkably calm and they quickly got the horses out of the wagon and into a roadside field. Amazingly, a slight scratch on the neck of one of the horses was the only sign of injury. The cause of the trouble was later diagnosed as a broken kingpin, that had allowed the wheel to slip from the axle.

As his success grew, Harvey was able to improve his facilities. When the opportunity arose to purchase a former pig farm at High Eldwick, he moved from his semi-detached house in Bingley to create what is now an ideal training site for horses.

He converted the intensive pig unit into loose boxes and built an indoor school. These provided good accommodation for the horses and the opportunity to train them adequately in poor weather. However, Harvey insists that any indoor training must be done with discretion and every hour that a horse spends inside must be balanced by the same amount outside, walking and jumping, to keep the horse alert and interested.

Harvey created a series of fences and obstacles around the farm, to allow the horses to canter round and jump for a period without stopping. In addition he used the excellent surrounding moorland for longer canters.

These facilities served Harvey well, and not only in the training sense. His farm, as he puts it, is situated right in the centre of the country and is convenient for motorways, thereby providing good access to show-jumping events, be they in Scotland, or the south of England. This also applies to the race meetings that Harvey now attends, for he is currently involved in the training of racehorses. He considers himself as a cog in the wheel of a training team, which, in addition to nurturing racehorses, also breaks-in and develops young horses for other owners. His wife, Sue, holds the trainer's licence, but they all work together with the sixty to seventy horses that are kept at the farm.

Harvey found the transition from jumping to racing quite hard,

Fountains Fell Tarn

but he enjoys his new challenge, particularly the training of young horses, which he finds very satisfying. The youngsters, he feels, can be developed into straight and reliable horses and can be easier dealt with than some older ones.

Training facilities have also been extended in the neighbouring fields, where tracks have been constructed, complete with fences, to accommodate the needs of racehorses. The training team feels that it now has resources that are second to none.

Harvey allowed me to photograph the horses in training and whilst I was so occupied, he was keeping a watchful eye on events and checking on the fitness of the horses. I could sense his concern for their welfare and he was very protective, asking me to keep at a discreet distance, so as not to frighten them.

I also gathered that careful attention must be paid to a horse's feeding routine. It obviously has a significant effect on their condition and the correct balance must be maintained. Harvey aimed at creating a condition that was just below total freshness, for his jumping horses. In his experience, when a horse is tired, he concentrates more, whereas a fresh horse can jump higher and wider, but does not concentrate to the same degree.

I asked Harvey which of his many show-jumping horses had been his favourite. He did not name one particular horse, but he admitted that he had a soft spot for Farmer's Boy, which had gained him recognition. It was a very careful animal, not the most talented, but always wanting to jump fences and extremely loyal. Harvey reckoned that if he had acquired it later in life it would have been a better horse. When he purchased him, Harvey knew very little about horses and they had to help each other as they went along.

Harvester, another of his favourites, he found to be a very genuine horse who never refused to jump. If there was only a ten percent chance of clearing a fence he would still have a go. A good, honest animal in Harvey's eyes.

Sanyo Sanmar, one of the famous Sanyo string of horses, was another that Harvey liked. He was bought as an old horse – old in years, but not in mileage. Before he was acquired he would not work for others, but Harvey got him going and moulded him into a good horse.

Harvey's career has left little time for other activities, but I did discover that he likes to visit the Yorkshire Dales when the rare opportunity arises. He holds Wharfedale in high esteem, particularly the Burnsall to Kettlewell section.

Although he does not have the time to extensively tour the Dales by car, there are several scenic routes within them that he likes to take. The steep and winding drive from Arncliffe, in Littondale, to Malham Tarn is one of his favourites. He enjoys the journey from Malham Tarn to Stainforth, in Ribblesdale, and onwards to the area around Penyghent. Another route that he likes to follow begins at Kettlewell and follows the narrow road that snakes up to Park Rash under the shadow of Great Whernside and continues over the watershed into Coverdale, where it descends to Leyburn, in Wensleydale.

As a youngster he spent many happy interludes on Malham Moor, at Tennant Gill Farm. The farmer had a trapping pony and Harvey liked to spend his holidays there. The Pennine Way skirts the farm and begins a gradual ascent of Fountains Fell. During the climb, which Harvey often made on horseback, it passes close to one of his best loved locations, the quiet and secluded Fountains Fell Tarn. Even though it is much smaller and more remote than Malham Tarn, it possesses a wild and untamed beauty.

Although Harvey's local travel has been restricted, show-jumping provided ample opportunity for world travel and of the many countries that he has had the good fortune to visit, there are two that stand out.

Mexico was a country that fascinated him. He was there for six weeks and really enjoyed himself. The reason for his lengthy stay, at the time of the 1968 Olympic Games, was due to him being sent out some weeks prior to the Games with the British team's horses. He was due to ride for the team and had been given the task of keeping an eye on the horses and assisting the grooms to get them acclimatised to the altitude of 7,000 feet. Harvey stayed in the Olympic village on the outskirts of Mexico City and, as there was an athletic track available, he thought that he ought to keep himself fit. Consequently, he got up at 6 a.m. each morning for a training run, but found the strain at that altitude quite remarkable. One morning his enthusiasm ran away with him. He trotted to the track as usual, only to find it unusually quiet. Many athletes trained early in the morning and by 7 a.m. the track was usually crowded, but that particular morning it was deserted. Harvey happened to look up at the clock above the track to find that it was quarter-past three! He rapidly returned to his room and jumped back into bed.

Harvey had been selected to jump in the individual event, the Grand Prix, alongside David Broome and Marion Coakes. Marion won silver on Stroller and David followed up with bronze on Mister Softee.

The same three riders were selected to represent Britain in the team event, the Grand Prix de Nations. Unfortunately, Stroller was eliminated in the second round of the competition for going over the time limit and this ended the team's hopes.

The British team manager was Sir Harry Llewellyn, for whom Harvey has the utmost respect. With his famous horse, Foxhunter, he laid the foundations for the sport in the modern era. Sir Harry became a hero in the 1952 Olympics, when he won the only British gold medal. His success captured the hearts of the British public when show-jumping had just begun to appear on the burgeoning television. Sir Harry is still alive and in his nineties.

Another country that Harvey enjoyed visiting was South Africa. He found it a wonderful place and he is especially pleased that so much anti-apartheid progress has been made in recent years. This can only be good for everyone, he feels.

In answer to my query regarding other sports, Harvey replied that he had never had ambitions to do anything other than show-jumping, which he has always been hooked on. This does not mean that he never watches other sports. He is fond of many, particularly cricket, and likes to see them on television, which, he feels, provides excellent coverage.

Harvey enjoyed playing cricket at school and he took part in the occasional game in the years that followed. On one occasion he turned out for a celebrity team, which was playing the England women's XI. It included many well-known names, not least of them being Gerald Harper, who, at that time, was starring in the Yorkshire Television series 'Hadleigh.' Harvey recalls that he took three wickets in the match.

I raised the thorny subject of officialdom, with which Harvey has had numerous problems. 'I have no regrets,' he replied. 'Everything I did came from the heart.' He obviously suffers no remorse over his legendary V-sign, for it has become a by-word in the annals of sporting history. In his book, *V is for Victory*, he gives a full account of the incident, which occurred during the final round of the British Jumping Derby at Hickstead in 1971. Harvey had won the competition the previous year and was hoping to retain the cup for the second year running. He was riding Mattie Brown, who unfortunately dislodged a pole at Devil's Dyke, a difficult combination fence, during the first round. As the pole fell, a cheer went up from the balcony overlooking the fence, which convinced him that its occupants did not want him to win. He reckoned that it took a strange sort of person to applaud when a horse was doing his best, but happened to make a mistake, and it had the effect of making Harvey doubly determined to win. He reached the final jump-off, beat the competition and emerged triumphant. A mixture of pleasure and relief engulfed him and, on the spur of the moment, he raised two fingers of his right hand in the direction of the offending balcony overlooking Devil's Dyke. It was a V for Victory, that was meant to show how delighted he was that Mattie Brown had become the first horse to win the British Jumping Derby in successive years.

If it was interpreted as 'up you' by those on the balcony, who had wanted Mattie Brown to lose, that was fair enough, but the gesture was meant to be light-hearted and the crowd received it as such. If it had been made offensively, they would have reacted against it. As for Harvey, if the incident had really upset him, he would not have the V-sign displayed on his back door!

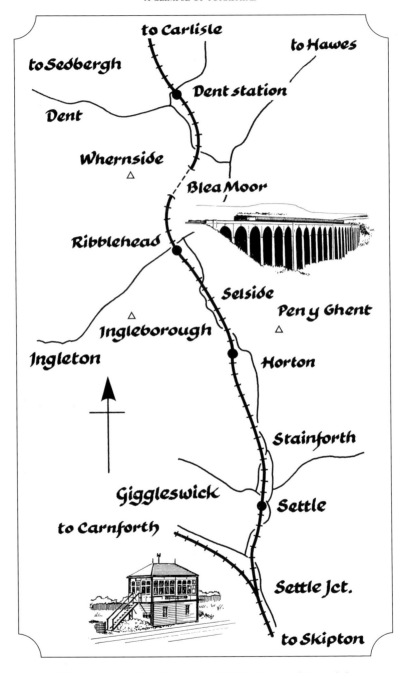

The Settle-Carlisle Railway in Ribblesdale and Dentdale

CHAPTER TWO

The Settle-Carlisle Railway in Ribblesdale and Dentdale

In the 1980's the crumbling limestone arches of the mighty Ribblehead Viaduct posed a major threat to the Settle-Carlisle Railway. British Rail applied to the Secretary of State for Transport for permission to close the line, which, in their opinion, was no longer commercially viable. They had reckoned without the perseverance of the organisation which had been formed to fight the closure, the Friends of the Settle-Carlisle Railway, whose members were determined that a vital part of Britain's railway heritage would not die. For five years these enthusiasts battled against threatened closure, believing that the Settle-Carlisle, completed in 1876, embodied much more than a mere seventy-two miles of track that links the market town of Settle with the strategic border city of Carlisle.

The campaign was also well targeted in the political arena. Lobbying was conducted in Westminster and an all-party committee of MP's was established to help save the line.

Thankfully, British Rail's plans were thwarted, the greatest of the line's viaducts was repaired and the death sentence was averted. Hopefully, this served as a lesson to those whose sole consideration in any enterprise is money. This is vital of course, but so is the preservation of our traditions and cultural legacies. The Settle-Carlisle is a tribute to the foresight of its planners and the skill and hard graft of its builders, that should not be forgotten. With closure prevented, the role of the Friends of the Settle-Carlisle was changed to one of encouragement for, and development of, the line.

The Settle-Carlisle was inaugurated by the Midland Railway Company as a fast, all-weather route to Scotland. A major development in the North, it brought the company into close partnership with the Glasgow and South Western Company and also a part interest in the steamship service from Stranraer to Larne. It brought other benefits, which included some of its stations becoming a focal point for the rural, isolated communities that they served. For example, at Garsdale, church services were held in the waiting room, a library was provided for railway families and dances took place in the tank house. Refreshments were also served in a disused railway carriage.

Times have changed since the heady days of steam and those tight-knit communities. Diesel trains now frequent the Settle-Carlisle, which continues to brave rugged terrain and fierce, unpredictable weather as it traverses wild moors and inspiring dales. The initial part of its journey, where it cuts through upper Ribblesdale, burrows beneath Blea Moor and reaches Dentdale, is covered in this chapter.

Alfred Wainwright was a great admirer of Settle and the distinctive limestone country that surrounds it. He was one amongst many and it certainly forms a fitting starting point, set beneath rugged Castlebergh, one of the numerous sculptured outcrops that are a feature of the local Craven Hills. Take the zig-zag path to its crest and you will enjoy a 'bird's-eye' view of the town and the surrounding Ribblesdale landscape in return for your exertions. A prominent flagpole was erected on its pinnacle at the time of Queen Victoria's coronation and a rippling flag can often be seen, flying from it, by the crowds that wander through the narrow streets and alleyways that lie beneath.

Settle has been a market town and popular meeting place since the granting of its charter in 1249. It formerly lay on the busy A 65 road that runs from Skipton to Kendal, but it is now thankfully by-passed, thus ensuring peace from the traffic that roars towards Lakeland. However, its centre is usually bristling with cars that bring visitors from a wide area. On market days, stalls occupy the square under the watchful gaze of the Shambles, the tasteful stone-built premises, which, like their namesakes in York, were originally occupied by butchers.

Amongst the many notable buildings in the town, two are particularly prominent. These are the Folly and Ye Naked Man Café. The former is an expertly crafted seventeenth-century structure, built by Richard Preston, which is particularly enhanced by its ornate front doorway. The ravages wreaked upon its delicate profile by the elements, is soon be combated by financial assistance. A successful bid has been made by the North Craven Building Preservation Trust for money from the Heritage Lottery Fund, to rescue the Grade 1 Listed Building.

Settle market square

View of Penyghent from Horton in Ribblesdale station

View of Dentdale from Blea Moor

Arten Gill Viaduct, Dentdale

The café displays a seventeenth-century carved figure, from which its name is derived, and it formerly had a counterpart, Ye Naked Woman Inn in the nearby village of Langcliffe. This hostelry has gone but a carved figure remains on a stone high on a house front, discreetly covered with a panel bearing the inscription '1660 ISMS.'

The limestone scars to the north and east of Settle are riddled with fissures and caves, the most famous of these being Victoria Cave in Langcliffe Scar. It was located in 1838 by Michael Horner, who crawled into its eerie chamber that had lain untouched since Roman times. An extensive excavation was undertaken and the remains of early man and animals were unearthed. Evidence revealed that elephant, rhinoceros and hippopotamus once roamed the area during the Great Inter-Glacial Period. At the end of the Ice Age came the fox, reindeer and badger, until eventually, man arrived. The remains of weapons and tools, which were used by Mesolithic hunters, were found. Iron Age man, who probably used the cave for refuge at the time of the Romans, left behind examples of Celtic jewellery and other artefacts.

Upper Ribblesdale has harboured its share of industry and evidence of this is clearly visible as the Settle-Carlisle progresses up the valley towards Horton-in-Ribblesdale. Mills, quarries and a lime works feature prominently around the initial section of the railway, proving that the dale was once a place of thriving and hard-working communities. Several mills still line the river between Settle and Stainforth, their gaunt chimneys a reminder of the days when cotton was produced in the valley. Langcliffe Mill and its adjacent cluster of dwellings mark the original site of the village of Langcliffe, which was sacked during a punitive Scottish raid in 1318 and, consequently, was moved to its present site on the opposite side of the main road that runs from Settle to Ribblehead. It is an attractive village that contains a dainty drinking fountain, set in a tiny cobbled square and boasts an elegant Hall, occupied for many years by the Dawson family. Geoffrey Dawson, who lived there in the early part of the century, was editor of *The Times* for twenty-six years.

The first of the quarries that disfigure the landscape appears beyond Langcliffe, where the craggy face of Winskill Scar has been gouged by the Craven Lime Company, which operated the site until it was abandoned in 1940. The limestone hewn from the escarpment was smelted in the nearby kiln, which remains largely intact. It is

Ribblehead Viaduct

possible to enter its dark and dank confines, that are relieved only by the feeble shafts of light which penetrate the numerous openings in its extremely thick walls.

The railway, road and river keep in close contact as they cut through this narrow section of the dale and they soon pass the quiet village of Stainforth. Typical of many such well-preserved settlements, its narrow streets are bordered by stimulating gardens and neat stone cottages. The Church of St. Peter stands on the edge of the village, surrounded by lush meadows that blaze with colour when the wild flowers are in bloom. The view across the valley from the churchyard is dominated by the hump of Smearsett Scar, which is the first of many delightful limestone formations that can be enjoyed on a walk from Stainforth to the hamlet of Feizor and onwards to Austwick and Clapham. This journey follows what was part of the old packhorse route from York to Lancaster.

The Ribble is crossed at the outset of this walk by a rounded stone bridge that is now in the care of the National Trust. It was built in the late seventeenth century by Samuel Watson, who also erected nearby Knight Stainforth Hall, which stands amongst a group of farms that comprise the hamlet of Little Stainforth. The impressive

Blea Moor Tunnel

three-storied hall derives its name from four knights of chivalry, or Knight's Templars, who lived in the settlement.

The Settle-Carlisle progresses through the valley, flanked by rolling farmland and sheep pastures that cover the limestone foothills. Moorland sweeps upwards to Moughton Scar in the west and Penyghent in the east. The railway crosses and re-crosses the meandering Ribble by means of sturdy bridges that carry it high above the dancing water that has not travelled far from its gathering grounds at Ribblehead. The actual source of this significant river, which flows to the sea beyond Preston, has long been the subject of debate. There are several possibilities, the main one being the point where the dale road, that we are following, meets the Ingleton to Hawes road within sight of Ribblehead Viaduct. However, there is a strong flow of water at this location and the Ordnance Survey denotes a nearby cave, adjacent to the road, as the source. Another choice is the head of the Cam Beck, the secondary tributary of the Ribble, whilst others favour the springs of Gayle Beck that lie in Newby Head Pasture.

As Helwith Bridge is approached, the dominant dome of Penyghent rises from the upper Ribblesdale landscape like a

Water crane near Blea Moor

weathered colossus. Its rounded contour, as seen from this perspective, masks the distinctive cut-away profile of its southern ridge, but its steep slopes make a compelling sight.

The compact settlements of Helwith Bridge and its neighbour, Studfold are synonymous with stone quarrying. They lie in the shadow of the great upthrust of Moughton Scar, that is partly eaten away by the removal of innumerable tons of limestone and slate. 'Helwith' is a Norse word, meaning 'ford paved with flat stones,' which signifies that the great slabs of slate, for which Moughton Scar is renowned, have been quarried since those times. They have served a variety of purposes, including paving, doorsteps, gateposts and even partitions in byres. The remarkable access to two kinds of stone in the quarry is due to the Craven Fault, which has exposed Silurian slates beneath the band of limestone.

At Helwith Bridge, the course of the river was slightly altered during the construction of the railway, a section of which stands on the site of the original riverbed. The Ribble's course had undergone a much more dramatic alteration at this point many centuries earlier, when it swung southwards onto its present line. Originally it veered to the west and into Wharfe Gill to become a tributary of the Lune.

Snow near Dent station

Two miles up-dale from Helwith Bridge lies Horton-in-Ribblesdale, in the heart of 'Three Peaks Country.' It houses the Penyghent Café, the popular starting and finishing point of the twenty-five-mile walk that encompasses Penyghent, Whernside and Ingleborough. Multitudes of walkers set out expectantly to conquer this gruelling challenge, some fall by the wayside, but the majority make a triumphant return to the café to enjoy a celebratory pint mug of tea and to re-live the experience with their companions.

I have a soft spot for the Penyghent Café, for it was from there that I embarked on my first ever long-distance walk, around the Three Peaks. The following year I stayed overnight in one of a row of nearby cottages, situated opposite the Crown Hotel, whilst walking the Pennine Way. I was made very welcome and the luxurious bed ensured that I enjoyed one of the soundest night's sleep of the complete walk. On that particular day I had walked from Malham, which involved climbing Fountains Fell and Penyghent on the way; an itinerary guaranteed to ensure the sleep of the innocent.

The hump of Penyghent has changed its shape by the time Horton is reached. The railway station offers a superb full-length view of the 'sleeping lion,' as it is otherwise known. It is easy to see why it has earned that nickname, from the shape of its dramatic profile that fills the horizon on the opposite side of the valley.

The village of Horton is indicative of the changing face of upper Ribblesdale throughout the years. Enduring Yeoman farmhouses mingle with Victorian terraces, built during the early days of the railway, and houses of a later vintage, occupied by quarry workers.

Beecroft Quarry scars the landscape to the west of the village and its great gash can be plainly seen from the summit of Penyghent. Lime works were installed at Beecroft in 1887 by Settle Limes Ltd. and mechanisation was introduced, utilising gas-fired kilns and a giant crusher, that could reduce massive blocks of limestone to small pieces. At that time Horton station had four and a half miles of sidings and possibly handled more tonnage of stone than any station of comparable size in the country.

The noise and activity has diminished and the station quietly straddles the once busy line, its trim stone buildings still displaying the red and white paintwork, familiar to rail travellers for decades. Neat flowerbeds border the platforms, obviously well tended by the station staff. When the railways were in full swing, most stations had gardens of which their custodians were justly proud. In fact, there was significant rivalry, for prizes were awarded for the most attractive and best-kept of them.

As the Settle-Carlisle leaves Horton it steers towards the tiny hamlet of Selside and beyond, the next station at Ribblehead. It was planned to build a station at Selside in the early days of the line, but it never materialised and the settlement had to be content with a signal box. This holds the distinction of being one of the first main line boxes to be fully manned by women during the Second World War. These stalwart ladies must have been self-assured, because signal boxes can be frightening places when you are on your own at night. In fact, during that conflict, it was believed that remote areas, such as that surrounding Ribblehead, could be ideal for dropping airborne invaders.

Penyghent is an ever-present companion during this stage of the journey. It crowns the skyline to the east until Ribblehead is reached. The landscape widens beyond Selside and the drumlins, which coat the valley-floor, become easily apparent. This collection of small, rounded humps, that resembles a rippling ocean, consist of glacial debris, deposited by a glacier which progressed along the valley during the last Ice Age.

Whilst trains negotiate a broad curve in the track, during their approach to Ribblehead, the huge bastion of Whernside is revealed, an imposing wall of rock, which appears to lie directly in their path. Fortunately, the track skirts its extensive brooding profile, under which squats what is probably the finest feature of the Settle-Carlisle, the Ribblehead Viaduct. Lying just beyond Ribblehead station, this quarter-mile-long structure forms a compelling landmark, its twenty-four towering arches straddling low-lying Batty Moss, a depression that shelters beneath the course foothills of Whernside.

Although commonly referred to as Ribblehead Viaduct, its correct name is Batty Moss and it is shown as such on the Ordnance Survey map of the area. At one time, a hundred trains passed over it, in either direction, each day. The bleak and cheerless basin, in which the viaduct lies, is at the mercy of the elements and the wind has been known to prevent trains from crossing the exposed structure. Westerly gales funnel between Whernside and nearby Ingleborough and the arches seem to suck the wind through them. The tale is told of a ganger who crossed the viaduct in a high wind, which snatched the cap from his head, blew it under one of the arches and back onto his head. It landed the wrong way round and jokingly, the man declared, 'Well, you can't have everything.'

At Ribblehead station, sheeters or 'gale men,' as they were known, were employed to ensure that sheets were securely fixed to the freight wagons during rough weather, to prevent them from being blown away when the train crossed the viaduct.

This halt also became a weather station in 1938 and a rain gauge was installed in 1954. The year that the gauge was installed, a bucket would have been more appropriate, for 110 inches of rain fell, including five inches in one day. All stationmasters held positions of respect and the one at this particular station must have been highly regarded, for he had the dual responsibility for the safe passage of trains and for measuring the elements.

The construction of the viaduct was a magnificent feat, considering its isolated location and unpredictable weather. Many shanty towns sprang up in the surrounding area, to house the navvies, when work commenced in 1869. Conditions were harsh and primitive. Many workers succumbed to illness and disease and there were frequent accidents, which claimed many lives. These camps were given names, some relating to the Crimean War, such as, Inkerman and Sebastopol. Others had religious connotations,

Ingleborough

namely, Jerusalem, Jericho and Salt Lake. Nearby railway cottages were named after some of the camps. Batty Green, the site of the viaduct, had, in addition to its camp, a school, post office, library, mission and a small hospital that was constructed to combat a smallpox epidemic.

Another challenge faced the railway builders, beyond Ribblehead. This was the crossing of desolate Blea Moor, which involved the creation of a tunnel, more than a mile in length. A broad track leads over the moor and a section of it follows the line of the tunnel, which can be easily traced by the ventilation shafts that sprout from the moorland like grimy pepper pots. These played a vital role in exhausting smoke and fumes from the claustrophobic confines of the tunnel, but, even with the aid of these, conditions were often intolerable. Old railwaymen and tunnelmen look back on the tunnel with dread. It was normally dripping wet, creating prodigious icicles in winter, that were smashed as trains thundered through. Workers got absolutely black from the grime and soot, up to half an inch thick, that lined the tunnel walls. They were often nearly choked by the smoke, which often took a long time to clear and would waft back and forth along the tunnel. Conditions were so bad that the rails had to be replaced every four years because of damage by water and sulphur.

The line curves to the north as it ventures onto Blea Moor, where it soon passes the marooned signal box, which can only be reached

Steam train standing in station

by track from Ribblehead. It stands alone in a wasteland of heath, grazed by hardy sheep that crop the course vegetation. Provisions are supplied by the passing trains. The adjacent house is now a crumbling shell and it has rather optimistically been put on the market recently, for a few thousand pounds.

Signalmen earn their keep at Blea Moor signal box, particularly in the harsh winters, when it is virtually inaccessible. In 1947 a signalman walked to work over walls that were buried under the deep snow. The Horners, father and son, worked there for many years and Mr. Horner senior travelled by bicycle from Salt Lake, the cottages named after the shanty town. Despite the loneliness, they were always kept busy watering the frequent locomotives and chatting to the crews as they changed over.

On the approach to the tunnel the daunting mass of Whernside looms over the Settle-Carlisle. Lively streams tumble down its lower slopes and waterfalls cascade at Force Gill, close to the point where the Three Peaks path crosses the line. Walkers can often be observed, as they commence the long and energy-sapping pull to the summit of Whernside.

Beyond this point, a black void appears and within seconds daylight vanishes as Blea Moor tunnel is entered and the only sound is the steady beat of the wheels on the track. A pinpoint of light emerges and gradually expands until the train rushes from the eerie blackness and into the striking landscape of Dentdale.

Meanwhile, the track that follows the line of ventilation shafts across Blea Moor, climbs to its crest, where an exciting vista of dales and hills unfolds. The view alone justifies the climb, but, as you strain up the testing slope, the wild beauty of this lonely expanse becomes distinctly apparent.

A thick forest guards the entrance to Dentdale and, when a descent is made into it, a dramatic picture of the tunnel exit is revealed through a tapering avenue of pines. On one occasion, when I entered the depths of the forest, I was fortunate to see a train disappear, as if by magic, into the tunnel.

The railway embarks on a high-level traverse around the head of the verdant dale. Eschewing the valley floor, it contours the hillsides, on a man-made ledge, crossing two elevated viaducts as it does so. The line at this point offers superb views of the gentle valley that lies beneath it.

One of the quieter of the Yorkshire Dales, Dentdale offers peace and contentment, amidst scenery of a unique character. A drive through the upper dale is akin to following a leafy lane, with the sparkling River Dee in close attendance. It is traversed by a narrow road from Newby Head, on the Ingleton to Hawes road, that passes beneath Dent Head Viaduct. From there it traces a winding course to the tiny settlements of Stone House and Cowgill. At the time of the construction of Ribblehead Viaduct, the churchyard at Cowgill overflowed with the unmarked graves of unfortunate navvies.

In the district remain many household features made from the famous Dent marble, the distinctive limestone that was quarried locally and was used for the construction of Dent Head and Arten Gill viaducts. Stone House Marble Works were renowned until the removal of the import tariff on Italian marble killed the local trade. Staircases at the Inns of Court and Cartwright Hall in Bradford display the beauty of Dent marble. Cowgill and Stone House retain chimney-pieces and chess tables skilfully made from this material, whose highly-polished surface often revealed patterns created by fossils.

By the mid-nineteenth century, poverty and de-population had overtaken the dale. Stone House Marble Works provided some employment, but the knitting trade, which had been the mainstay of the area, declined. The coming of the Settle-Carlisle was a godsend, for it afforded work to the stricken valley between 1869 and 1876.

A steep, rutted track climbs from the valley bottom and passes beneath Arten Gill Viaduct, on its way to the bleak moorland that separates Great Knoutberry Hill and Wold Fell. Quarrymen and miners trod this demanding path on their way to work, which necessitated hard graft and long hours. At the head of Arten Gill, the track meets the old road from Dentdale to Hawes, which continues as a well-defined track to Widdale, where the modern metalled road from Ingleton to Hawes is joined.

A little farther along the valley, at Lea Yeat, near Cowgill, a metalled road, formerly known as the 'coal road,' rises to Dent station, perched high on the hillside. It is so called because it formerly led to the coal mines on the lower slopes of Great Knoutberry Hill. This forms another section of the old road from Dentdale to Hawes that contours Pike Edge, as a green lane, to reach the head of Arten Gill.

Dent station is the highest main line station in England, at 1150 feet above sea level. It is over four miles from the village of Dent, the largest settlement in the dale and its isolated and elevated position make it vulnerable to the vagaries of the weather. During the winter of 1947, the railway around Dent station was impassable for eight weeks. The snow lay so deep at the station itself, that a man is reputed to have walked on the buried roof of the waiting room, not realising that it was there. A railway official raised a smile, despite the arctic conditions, by removing his raincoat, which was frozen solid, and standing it on the floor of the waiting room.

Snow cabins and fences were built earlier in the century to combat the fierce snowfalls. The cabins were stone-built and primarily for the use of men employed in snow clearing. There was a saying on the line at that time; 'During fog or snow, into the cabin you must go.' Two long sleeper fences were constructed above the line, in addition to the retaining wall, in an effort to keep the drifting snow in check. Unfortunately, when the blizzards were in full force, the fences proved inadequate.

On this chilly note, our journey on the Settle-Carlisle draws to a close. We leave the line as it says farewell to Dentdale and enters Rise Hill tunnel. The highest point of the railway, 1169 feet, lies a few miles hence, at Ais Gill Summit. In the days of steam, the fireman would be furiously shovelling coal into the furnace, to ensure that his train completed the long pull from Settle to the summit, known as the 'Drag.' When that objective was reached, he could relax and enjoy the long descent to Carlisle.

Belle View Cottage

CHAPTER THREE
Hannah – Nine Years On

I knocked expectantly on the door of Belle View Cottage, a trim, white-walled building that overlooks the quiet main street of the pleasant village of Cotherstone. In my search for the cottage I had passed the nearby village green and admired rows of colourful daffodils straddling the tiny brook that bisects it. A polite and friendly voice, which I immediately recognised as that of Hannah Hauxwell, filtered through an open bedroom window and enquired if I would mind waiting for a moment. An elderly gentleman passed as I stood, feeling rather self-conscious, outside the door. Half-expecting an enquiry concerning my business there, I received, instead, a cheerful greeting. We exchanged pleasantries and when I asked about his health, he replied, with a twinkle in his eye, that he was keeping the undertaker on hold.

As I waited, I wondered what lay behind the door of Hannah's abode since leaving the harsh conditions that she had endured on her farm at Low Birk Hatt. A few moments later I found out when she politely invited me through the half-open door and gave me a very friendly greeting. It proved quite a squeeze to get through the constricted doorway, obstructed as it was by articles that had piled up within it. I was guided into her compact living kitchen, where it was just possible to negotiate a path to two chairs positioned amongst a sea of boxes, parcels and assorted bric-a-brac that filled the room.

A passage from *Daughter of the Dales* came to mind, where she had voiced her ambition, when leaving Low Birk Hatt, to sort out the confusion in which she lived. 'It won't be easy, because of my hoarding instinct' Hannah had said, in 1989, when embarking on a five-year plan to create a tidy living environment. From first impressions she was fighting a losing battle, for her situation appeared just as chaotic as I remembered from scenes in her farmhouse that were featured on television in *A Winter Too Many*. I became anxious to begin an immediate tidying operation, which I don't think Hannah would have appreciated and I am sure that she is not disordered through choice. However, I reasoned that if she had a neat and tidy home, perhaps she would not be the outstanding character that she is.

As we squeezed ourselves into the chairs, conveniently placed near the gas central heating boiler, which Hannah calls 'The Great One', I soon began to realise that what she lacks in tidiness is far outweighed by her open and generous nature and innate kindness. Completely unaffected by her fame, she lives as she always has, quietly, simply and untouched by affectation. In her soft-spoken, gentle manner, she willingly submitted to my enquiries concerning her life since moving down the valley to Cotherstone. No doubt she had been asked countless such questions by media representatives who had beaten a path to her door, but she patiently responded to mine for more than two hours.

Hannah has been described as the 'First Lady of the Dales', an accolade that she accepts with appreciation. Purists may argue that her 'home' dale, Baldersdale, has been annexed to County Durham, but Barry Cockcroft, who is responsible for her projection into the public eye, through his books and television documentaries, eschews this jaundiced view. In *Seasons of My Life,* he refers to Baldersdale as a 'Classic Yorkshire Dale' and elaborates, 'It is a Yorkshire dale in the classic sense with sweeping contours and a fierce beauty on the grand scale, although in recent years it has been placed in County Durham (not that locals pay any attention to such cultural vandalism).'

In response to my query of how life at Belle Vue Cottage compared to that at Low Birk Hatt, Hannah replied, 'better in some respects, worse in others'. She likes the modern conveniences provided in the cottage, such as running water and washing facilities, but misses the open spaces and the 'sands of the Mississippi,' her name for the shore of Blackton Reservoir, where she used to wash her clothes. Despite the rigours of washing garments and household linen in its chill waters, she found the setting therapeutic, as she does all those that surround water.

The view from the farm towards the gnarled crag of Goldsborough, which lies across Blackton Reservoir, is, in her opinion, one of sheer delight. Despite the lure of this enchanting view, Hannah has never returned to her former dwelling, for it holds too many bitter-sweet memories. In fact, when I suggested featuring an illustration of another of her favourite views – across the reservoir from the byre to the distinctive Clove Lodge – she recoiled, stressing that it would be too upsetting.

High Force

Amongst the other things that she misses are the wild flowers and her beloved animals. She loved the garlands of wild roses that encompass Hury Reservoir and the foxgloves and primroses that flourish in the lanes and fields around the farm. Another of her delights was to smell the hawthorn and rowan tree blossom that hangs in the scented air of upper Baldersdale. Her animal 'friends', as she describes them, were numerous. She particularly misses Rosa, her cow, which was cared for by a friend and neighbour after her move. Sadly, Rosa lost her teeth and, unable to eat properly, soon died. Hannah had a great affinity with her cows and the other 'beasts of the field', as she calls them. She turned to them for companionship and even for conversation! Rosa's mother, 'Her Ladyship', as she was named, became a constant companion for fourteen years.

The pigs, that rooted in the Baldersdale earth around the farm when Hannah was a child, were held in considerable esteem. Contrary to popular belief that they are dirty animals, she found some to have clean habits, in fact, one pig kept its bed and toilet places quite separate.

No dales farm is complete without its brood of dogs and these loyal, hard-working animals have always been close to Hannah's heart. Amongst the many that she has loved and cared for, her favourite was Chip, a black and white Border collie. She describes this affectionate companion as possessing a particularly nice nature and wonderful brown eyes.

Whilst on the subject of dogs, without any prompting, she repeated some verses of a poem that she had learned at school which expressed the depth of feeling that she has for them. This was not the only occasion that I was treated to an impromptu recital of poetry and I discovered that it is one of her passions. Her eyes shone as she related a passage from another poem remembered from childhood, about a donkey called Nicholas Nye, adding that she particularly likes poems that rhyme.

Her grandfather, James Hauxwell, inspired Hannah's enjoyment of poetry with his frequent recitals of poems and nursery rhymes. When it was the turn of *The House That Jack Built* he used to say that the 'maiden all forlorn' was Hannah herself. She loved her Granda, as she called him, despite his wild streak and his liking for drink. He made her feel happy. She will never forget another of his attributes, his lovely handwriting, or his rendition of Byron's *Vision of Belshazzar*, its opening verse never failing to move her.

> The King was on his throne
> The Satraps throng'd the hall;
> A thousand bright lamps shone
> O'er that high festival.
> A thousand cups of gold,
> In Judah deem'd divine –
> Jehovah's vessels hold
> The godless Heathen's wine!

Amongst other poems that Hannah loved to hear him recite were *Belshazzar's Feast, Bethjellet,* which she found a very sad story and *The Arab's Farewell to his Steed.* She gave a rendition of the latter

Hannah at the 'meeting of the waters' in Teesdale

The village green, Cotherstone

Pennine Way walkers passing Widdybank Farm, Upper Teesdale

Kirkcarrion, Lunedale

poem at the Baldersdale Methodist chapel that she regularly attended. On the occasion of the annual Chapel Anniversary, it was always overflowing with people from all parts of the dale.

According to Hannah, the locality has produced several accomplished poets Among those that she admired were Richard Watson, a lead-miner from Middleton in Teesdale, William Longstaffe of Mickleton and Walter Bayles, a distant relative on her father's side of the family. Another relative of hers, Jack Robinson, is similarly gifted and he has written several poems about Hannah. He was landlord of the Rose and Crown, in nearby Mickleton, for many years and is now retired.

Hannah has numerous artistic leanings, but admits to weakness in arithmetic and spelling, the latter developing in recent years. To her profound regret she frequently has to consult 'her friend' the dictionary. She loves music, a trait inherited from her mother, who was a fine organist. Her mother's treasured organ, that Hannah cannot bear to part with, will always occupy pride of place in her home. In fact there are three organs in her overcrowded cottage. Sadly, none of these are in working order. The electric organ, which she bought as a present to herself, is currently awaiting repair and is secreted in a corner of one of the rooms, silently awaiting a new lease of life.

An enthusiastic organist, Hannah wishes that she could be as proficient as her mother was. Her other ambition is to own a large and formidable model, the type that can virtually lift the roof, with a deep tone that can replicate a 'big-band' sound. I could visualise her rising happily from the depths of an orchestra pit, jauntily tinkling the myriad keys of a booming theatre organ, her feet pumping the pedals with great gusto.

Hannah has clearly missed her true vocation. I am convinced that she would have loved a career as an instrumentalist. At home on either piano or organ, she would have relished the opportunity to emulate the two Reginalds, Dixon and Forte, her idols of the theatre organ era.

By way of consolation, she appears content to enjoy the occasional workout on the organ, or listen to music on the radio. Hannah loves the dance orchestras that have broadcast over the years, such as Henry Hall, Geraldo and Joe Loss. Alan Dell's regular programme was a particular favourite and it is sorely missed.

The broad spectrum of her musical tastes extends from ragtime to opera. Giuseppe Verdi, the most popular Italian composer of the nineteenth century, is, in her estimation, the greatest of them all.

Whilst on her international travels following her emergence as a 'celebrity,' Hannah was privileged to visit the Paris Opera House whilst *Giselle* was in rehearsal. She found the wonderful setting an unforgettable experience. On another occasion, during her stay at the Savoy Hotel in London, she enjoyed a lovely conversation with an Italian waiter, named Giovanni, who was also a great fan of Verdi.

It was a picture book, loaned by a neighbour, many years before her visit, which aroused Hannah's interest in Paris and she recalls singing the familiar *Last Time I Saw Paris* when she left school. She read a great deal about Paris and other great cities of the world and longed to see them. Until the golden opportunity arose to realise her dream, she had never been further than Loch Lomond on a day trip.

Of all her travels, which she enjoyed immensely, the visits to Paris, Vienna and Venice evoke the most vivid memories. The romantic architecture and resplendent façade of Paris she found most impressive, but when she visited the Louvre and saw the Mona Lisa, she found the famous painting dark and much smaller than she had imagined.

As an alternative to Hannah's isolated existence at Low Birk Hatt, the opportunity to travel was a godsend and she revelled in the sights that previously she could only read about. She was particularly thrilled by London, where she was even asked for her autograph by some of the crowd thronging the railings that surround Buckingham Palace. It was a very pleasing welcome to the Royal Garden Party, to which she had been invited. On that occasion, in honour of the Queen Mother's birthday, she sported a very decorous dress and a broad-brimmed floral hat, which made her feel like a real lady, as she mixed with the great and the accomplished.

I enquired about Hannah's local travels around Yorkshire and its Dales. In this respect she was indebted to three friends whom she visited in Crosshills, a village situated between Keighley and Skipton. The sisters took her on numerous trips by car, introducing her to places that would otherwise have been inaccessible. Ilkley, she remembers as a lovely town, busy and prosperous, its beginnings steeped in history. She was intrigued by its Roman connections and admired the impressive buildings that were formally hydros in the days when Ilkley was renowned for the healing properties of its water. During one visit to the spa town she recalls a glimpse of the dramatic

Cow and Calf rocks that stand sentinel over the town. On what Hannah remembers as a high-level ride she journeyed along minor roads from Ilkley to Keighley, passing Harvey Smith's farm along the way. She had often admired Harvey's show-jumping exploits on television, even though the excitement that the sport engendered frequently proved too much for her.

Hannah's travels around Yorkshire increased dramatically when she became a household name, for everyone wanted to meet her and she was in great demand for opening a variety of functions. Until that time, the attractions of her locality had provided ample rewards. In addition to beautiful Baldersdale she had the delights of the sparkling River Tees within easy reach. One of the most attractive water-courses in the country, it tumbles from the Cow Green reservoir in a mighty cascade known as Cauldron Snout and glides towards Middleton in Teesdale. A beautiful stretch of water, punctuated by striking waterfalls and spanned by Middleton's imposing bridge, which Hannah greatly admires, it flows alongside one of the most endearing sections of the Pennine Way footpath. As the river and track travel hand in hand from Middleton to Langdon Beck, great sheets of Whin Sill manifest themselves. A form of Dolerite, an extremely hard rock that intruded into the strata over a wide area of upper Teesdale, they are responsible for the remarkable waterfalls, most notable of which is High Force. Here an eighty-foot torrent rushes over a giant wall of impervious rock in a frenzy of foam, which causes Hannah to look upon it as 'one of nature's masterpieces.'

It is fitting that the Pennine Way passes Low Birk Hatt, for it brought a multitude of walkers virtually to Hannah's door when she lived there. This provided the opportunity for many a welcome chat whilst they enjoyed a brief respite from their daily battle with sore feet and hefty rucksacks. It was through one such walker that Hannah was 'discovered.' The friend of a Yorkshire Television researcher stopped for a conversation whilst walking the long-distance path and found Hannah so remarkable that he suggested to the researcher that she would be good material for a television documentary. This message was relayed to Barry Cockcroft and the legend of Hannah Hauxwell was born.

I was privileged to walk the Pennine Way in 1987, but unfortunately there was no sign of Hannah as I passed the farm. However, I had spent the previous night at nearby Baldersdale Youth

Middleton in Teesdale

Hostel and had discovered a little about Hannah's harsh existence from the young and capable warden, Richard Megson. I learned that he frequently helped Hannah, particularly during the winter, her most difficult time. He also attended to any electrical repairs that she required. These became necessary after her television exposure and the laying of cables by the North East Electricity Board. An electric cooker and a washing machine had been donated by her admirers and Hannah was grateful for the services of her good friend and neighbour who attended to the new-fangled conveniences that had entered her life. She remembers Richard as a very nice and obliging young man and he still corresponds with her. He is a keen cyclist and since leaving the Youth Hostel he has toured many countries, including America, Australia and New Zealand.

Hannah apologised for being unavailable when I passed her farm in 1987, indicating that she really enjoyed hearing Pennine Way walkers' comments regarding their ordeal. She remembers one lady who, as a complete novice, found it very strenuous and exhausting. Her husband, meanwhile, had no such problems and was seemingly oblivious to his poor wife's predicament. Hannah smiled as she recalled another walker, a very elegant and well-spoken gentleman, who was walking the footpath carrying an umbrella. This, I

The Lune Viaduct

explained, was preferable to the ballast that a young Canadian, who I met on the Pennine Way, was lugging. In addition to the normal gear in his rucksack, he had a fifteen-pound rock. When I enquired what possessed him to carry such an unnecessary burden, he replied, 'Well it's something to do.'

I was interested to discover how Hannah occupies her time when not indulging in her pastime of sitting by her window and watching the world go by. Apparently, she very rarely watches television, which, she feels, could be such a force for good instead of featuring many programmes that are unsuitable for family viewing. She mourns the demise of the old cinemas, where one could enjoy films that depicted a gentler era. Many of those old black and white dramas are remembered with affection, but she also considers humour to be an important ingredient. This is why she liked the film star and comic actor Alastair Sim, well known for his portrayal of the scatty headmistress in the *St Trinians* series of films. She also remembers a youthful George Cole, who appeared as the unforgettable 'spiv' in that hilarious series. George, who was taken under the wing of Alastair as a young and inexperienced youth, subsequently blossomed under the guidance of his mentor. He has since achieved immortality for his portrayal of the modern-day 'spiv', or wheeler-dealer, Arthur Daley in the television series *Minder*.

Those old films were, Hannah believes, like a breath of fresh air, as there was no reliance on violence or crudity. In her opinion, they reflect how life has changed with the passing years and how its pace has quickened. She observes that during the Second World War, no one thought twice about waiting for hours in long queues, whereas now people cannot bear to wait for a few moments at traffic lights.

Hannah enjoys listening to the radio, not only for its music, but also for its variety of programmes. This is her link with the events of the outside world, for she does not exhaustively read newspapers or magazines, due to difficulties with small print. She is, however, still an eager book-reader, a pastime that she has enjoyed since her schooldays.

Methodism and chapel have always played an important role in Hannah's life and will remain the bedrock on which her outlook on the world is built. She attends Cotherstone chapel for worship whenever she can, but still treasures the friendships that she formed at Baldersdale chapel in the days when it was a focal point within the dale. Hannah enjoys the numerous activities of the chapel Guild during the winter months, such as talks, slide-shows and concerts. She is also fond of the Cockfield Methodist Male Voice Choir and goes to hear them whenever the opportunity arises. A great believer in the importance of chapel to the fabric of family life, she feels that it promotes a good legacy and is the foundation upon which society is built.

I eventually took my leave of Hannah, after enjoying some refreshment that she insisted on providing, 'to sustain me during my homeward journey', was how she persuasively put it. As we said goodbye at the door I was again struck by the inner radiance that shone through her ragged façade – she still wears the same style of tattered clothing that is so characteristic of her farming days. What a shining example to us all, I thought, as I shook hands with the remarkable lady who possesses an unbreakable faith in the old values and portrays an innocence that defies denigration.

CHAPTER FOUR

The Leeds and Liverpool Canal in Airedale

Airedale is a valley of character and industry. Through the limestone landscapes of its upper reaches dances the unsullied River Aire, soon to be tamed as it journeys between banks that were once thickly lined with textile mills. The energetic river played an important role in the growth of the textile industry of the West Riding, its waters being frequently harnessed to provide much needed power. Today the industrial grime and pollution has receded, but industry and activity are still the hallmarks of Airedale and the river that provides its life-blood.

The dale also embodies a section of the Leeds and Liverpool Canal, that is the longest man-made waterway in Britain. It searches out the Aire Gap, a channel through the Pennines that offered a convenient passage to Lancashire when John Longbotham surveyed a possible route for a canal that would link the River Aire with the River Mersey in 1765.

The 127 mile waterway was begun in 1770 and construction commenced simultaneously at Leeds and Liverpool. During the first seven years, significant progress was achieved and the canal reached Wigan in the west and Gargrave in the east. Unfortunately, progress was halted due to lack of funding and the Yorkshire and Lancashire ends operated independently until the link up was finally achieved in 1816. This pioneering project had taken 46 years to complete, at a cost of £1,200,000, nearly five times the original estimate.

The prime movers in the construction of the canal were businessmen and landowners in the Bradford area, who required convenient access to the limestone quarries of the Craven district. Their aim was to bring supplies of limestone from Skipton to their coal mines round Bingley and Bradford, where it would be burnt to provide lime for building purposes and land improvement. By way of reciprocation, coal could be cheaply transported to the limestone quarries in order to reduce the price of lime used on the local grazing lands. The most significant benefit was the opportunity to distribute textile products to the expanding Lancashire ports and onwards to

The Leeds and Liverpool Canal – Bingley to Gargrave

foreign markets.

The canal brought prosperity to the towns through which it passed and in its heyday was one of the most successful trading arteries ever built. Today the trade has gone and it provides a range of recreational facilities. It is used by a multitude of pleasure craft and canal side leisure complexes have risen from the ashes of derelict wharves and warehouses. Some of its most interesting features, such as Bingley Five Rise Locks attract thousands of visitors each year.

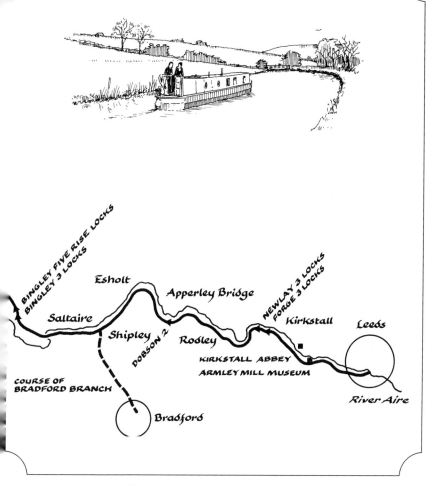

The Leeds and Liverpool Canal – Leeds to Bingley

There are excellent opportunities for canal users to discover Airedale's attractions, but you do not have to travel by boat to enjoy the valley's pleasant surroundings. It has a wide appeal for fishermen, walkers and those who enjoy a stroll along the canal towpath.

The following journey from Leeds to Gargrave will uncover many of the dale's attributes and historical traditions as we follow the canal and its close companion, the river, to the great rift in the Pennines.

It begins in the heart of the great city that was built on the cloth processing and clothing industries.

The home of Burton tailoring and the stall on Kirkgate Market that was the embryo of Marks and Spencer it is now an influential force in the nation's business and commercial sector.

Many people that throng City Square, under the gaze of high-rise blocks of glass and concrete, are unaware that the Leeds and Liverpool Canal begins a mere stone's throw away. Granary Wharf, or the Canal Basin, as it is known, hides behind the façade of Leeds City Station in the shadow of the 'Dark Arches' that lie beneath its formidable viaduct. Here amongst cobbled surrounds, renovated warehouses and a budding array of pristine commercial emporiums, the canal issues from the River Aire. If it were not for the plethora of new buildings that are changing the face of this oasis of tranquility, it would be easy to feel that one had stepped back in time. Cobbles underfoot, vaulted arches encompassing a warren of distinctive craft shops selling every kind of bric-a-brac, weekend market stalls and street entertainment, give the locality an olde worlde feel. It is reassuring that this atmosphere will survive, for plans are underway for a complete refurbishment of the site which will include bars, restaurants and an extension to the speciality shopping area.

An assortment of narrow boats, the most common craft of today, and launches, undulate at the moorings of the Canal Basin, many of them a decorous tribute to their owner's care and workmanship. Their appearance varies from the ornate to the merely functional and their names can be arranged in a scale of originality. 'Tranquility' evokes thoughts of lazy days of unhurried cruising, whereas, 'I'm Crackers Too' demonstrates a self-deprecating sense of humour.

A metal barge, with rust attacking its rivets, awaits an imaginary cargo, such as those formerly carried by the indigenous wooden barges of yesteryear. These predominantly coal-carrying craft were the workhorses of the canal, also transporting a diverse range of other commodities. American wheat for the Humberside mills, Australian wool from Liverpool, heading for Bradford and consignments of cocoa, sugar, nuts, dried fruit and caramel, bound for Rowntrees of York.

As the canal vacates the throbbing city centre, the clamour recedes and green borders replace stone and concrete. The retrospective skyline of thrusting hotels and office blocks is tempered by two ornate brick-built chimneys, which sprout from the former manufacturing complex of Tower Works. Built for Harding and Son, makers of pins, cards and combs for the textile industry, these works were a Victorian innovation. Its crowning glories, the two chimneys, are a tribute to Italian architecture. The smallest was erected in 1864 and was modelled on the Lamberti Tower in Verona. Its larger counterpart followed in 1899 and was based upon Giotto's campanile in Florence.

Hand in hand the canal and river carve a channel through the suburbs of Armley and Kirkstall. The Aire is punctuated by a series of weirs whose cascades present an energetic contrast to the sedate waters of the canal. These glide alternately between verdant, undulating banks, forbidding walls of rock and brick, or avenues of trees that protect the waterway from its urban surroundings. At one point, where the trees relent, the canal rides high above a panorama of factories and industrial estates. Yards crammed with container lorries and a vast accumulation of warehouses, bulging with goods, paint a scene of energetic activity.

At one point, two of the bleak factory walls, which line the canal, are relieved by colourful murals, painted by the Yorkshire Mural Artist Group. Entitled 'Fragments from the Post Industrial State 1981/ 84,' they provide an interesting diversion to people negotiating Oddy Lock. One cannot travel far along the Leeds and Liverpool Canal without encountering one of these obstacles, except on the level seventeen-mile section from Bingley to Gargrave. It is easy to smile at lock-users laboriously winding handles and pushing the heavy wooden bars that open and close the gates, but it demands sweat and toil to complete the manoeuvre. Anyone travelling the total length of the canal will have to perform it over ninety times.

As it does with many a scene, sunshine adds a new dimension to the canal and its surroundings. Under the sun's benevolent rays the brown water shimmers, its surface alive with intricate patterns woven by the scudding of myriad flies. Even the drabbest of backgrounds exhibits flashes of colour, be they mosses that cling to weathered walls or tiny plants that sprout from the smallest crevasses of the assortment of bridges that span the waterway. There are more than 250 of these structures, representing the changing styles of the past 220 years. Modern concrete hulks vie for pride of place with intricately fashioned iron and steel arrangements coated with measle-like rashes of rivets, and elegant stone-built arches of an earlier vintage.

Ornate and brightly-painted iron balustrades, that bedeck the

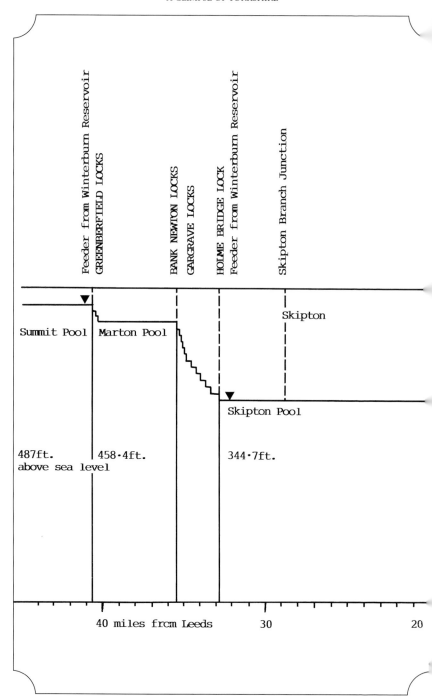

The Leeds and Liverpool Canal – Bingley to Gargrave – Side View

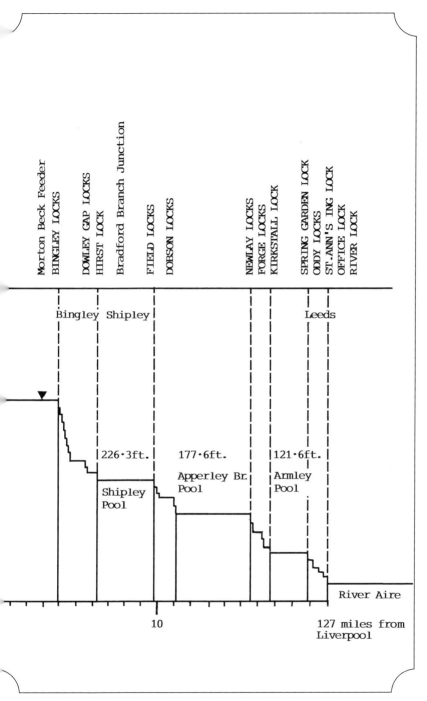

The Leeds and Liverpool Canal – Leeds to Bingley – Side View

functional concrete slab of an overpass, hail the approach to Armley Mills, which overlooks the canal towpath. Built in 1806, it represented the largest woolen mill in the world at that time. It currently houses the Leeds Industrial Museum, which aptly demonstrates the city's industrial heritage through its wide-ranging exhibits. In addition to the pivotal activities of wool textiles and tailoring, photography and printing are also featured. Devotees of steam engines, locomotives and waterwheels are also catered for.

Kirkstall has two notable landmarks adjacent to the canal, both of great historical significance. The first of them, Kirkstall Abbey, occupies a commanding site on the north bank of the river. Its blackened tower can be seen from the canal, rising from a cloak of woodland, with its great hollow window resembling an all-seeing eye. The sombre sandstone shell, still defying the ravages of time, represents one of the finest early monastic sites in Britain. Founded in 1152 by Henry de Lacey, Baron of Pontefract, it was run by the Cistercian Order for nearly 400 years, until its dissolution. A lasting reminder of the abbey's founder is the nearby thoroughfare named De Lacy Mount. The abbey and former gatehouse, now the Abbey House Museum, were gifted to the city by Colonel John North in 1889 and they continue to draw visitors from far and wide.

A little further up river stands Kirkstall Forge, adjacent to one of the mighty weirs, that was constructed in 1678 for the staggering sum, in those days, of £836, when extra water power was needed to operate a newly installed slitting mill for the iron bars that were the staple product of the forge. This innovation marked the introduction of automation into the manufacturing process, a remarkable feat for that era.

Production of ferrous metals was begun as early as 1200, when the monks of Kirkstall Abbey established a small forge on the site. It has evolved over the centuries into the extensive manufacturing complex that exists today. In 1863 the forge built a massive steam hammer, that was reputedly the second largest in the world, for a company in Sweden. Today, the firm which owns the complex, concentrates on the production of speciality axles. At the entrance to the site stands a gritstone obelisk, grimy with age, bearing a milestone on its base that indicates its position at the exact halfway point between London and Edinburgh – it being precisely 200 miles to each city.

As the outlying suburb of Calverley approaches, the landscape broadens after five miles of constraint and the mantle of urban sprawl is shrugged off. Canal and river cut through open fields and skirt ranging woodland as they head for Apperley Bridge. The ample towpath is a reminder of the days before steam power, when canal barges were pulled with horses. These hard-worked animals had to be unhitched when a tunnel was encountered and the bargees were required to 'leg it' through. This was achieved by lying on their backs on the deck and walking their feet along the tunnel walls. Horses were utilised until well into the first half of this century. Evidence of the long towropes that were used for horse-drawn craft remains to this day in the form of deep grooves worn into the masonry and metal of many locks.

Apperley Bridge is the site of a British Waterways depot and maintenance yard. This organisation is responsible for the upkeep of the canal and the dredgers that they operate can often be seen dipping their predatory beaks into the water to remove silt and debris.

The watery companions snake past Esholt sewage works and skirt the adjacent 'Emmerdale' village with its renowned 'Woolpack' Inn. The popular television series still attracts eager crowds to this attractive location, although, as I understand it, filming now takes place in a new and purpose built setting. Esholt is worthy of attention in its own right, for in addition to its pleasing stone cottages, it possesses a stately seventeenth-century manor house and a delightful church.

Arrival at the town of Shipley sees canal and river squeezed together once more for a passage between former warehouses and textile mills. A modern swing bridge heralds an important junction on the Leeds and Liverpool Canal where the scant remains of the Bradford Canal feed into it. The previously mentioned Bradford entrepreneurs were responsible for the construction of this three and a half miles long branch that provided a link with Forster Square, situated in the centre of the great wool city. Opened in 1774, it was a vital link in the distribution chain and it operated until 1922. It has virtually disappeared under tons of earth, but its line can still be detected in places.

Shipley is an industrial town, typical of many that lie in this part of Airedale. It is also the base for the Appollo Canal Cruises that operate from Shipley Wharf, a restored canalside complex, situated near to the town centre. From here, relaxing cruises can be enjoyed, enhanced by on-board refreshment. Prior to its current recreational use, the canal was the life-blood of the town, providing transport for the output of the mills and the supply of raw materials.

These facilities were equally vital to the famous Salts Mill, that stands a little further up the valley, surrounded by the model village of Saltaire, built by the mill's founder, Sir Titus Salt. The River Aire was utilised to drive the great turbines of Salts Mill, which was constructed in 1853. Sir Titus specialised in fabric made chiefly from alpaca, the hair of the South American Llama, and mohair, the coat of the Angora goat. Both of these commodities were brought to the mill by canal barge and the finished cloth distributed by the same means, until the onset of the railways. The use of such unique raw materials elevated Sir Titus from the boom and bust cycles suffered by the mills of Bradford. When he moved out of that city and built his mill, he also considered his workers, providing every amenity for them within the model village, except the wholesale consumption of alcohol. A moral reformer and a man of temperance, Sir Titus would not build a public house, with its associated rowdyism, but he did condone the operating of an off-licence.

The canal glides between the two ornate sections of Salts Mill, constructed in the Italianate style. Its two hundred and fifty feet high chimney dominates the surrounding landscape, a towering monument to the imagination and accomplishment of its creator. Things may have been different today if the buildings had been allowed to decay, as they were in danger of doing in the 1980's. The mill was saved by another man of vision, Jonathan Silver, who, through his company, Salts Estates Ltd. acquired the complex and gave it new life. Today it is a base for commercial, cultural and artistic activities, in addition to providing private accommodation. The centre-piece of the rejuvenated mill is the 1853 Gallery that contains many exhibits by David Hockney, the Bradford-born artist.

I am sure that if Sir Titus, whose body lies in the family mausoleum, on the south side of the United Reformed Church, which he also built, could see his creation in its present award-winning state, he would be well pleased.

Colourful gardens and rolling lawns flank the canal as it passes Roberts Park, another amenity provided for the workers of Salts Mill. Its relaxing surroundings still provide a quiet haven for visitors and the people of Saltaire.

As it courses through scenic Hirst Wood, the canal heads for the

The Leeds and Liverpool Canal near Leeds City centre

Salts Mill, Saltaire

Bingley Five Rise Locks

The Springs Branch, Skipton

township of Bingley, home to the familiar Damart Mill. Built in 1871, its prominent chimney smiles benignly at the waterway that passes beneath its shadow. Many such chimneys monopolised the skyline of Bingley when the textile trade was flourishing, but today the town busies itself with manufacturing and commercial interests. The headquarters of the Bradford and Bingley Building Society are located here and valuable research is carried out at the highly successful Sports Turf Research Institute, situated in the extensive grounds of Bingley St. Ives. The once well-utilised river is now allowed peaceful passage through the town and an attractive riverside walk has been created. Shapely Ireland Bridge straddles the Aire within sight of a familiar feature of the valley, a man-made step in the water, created to drive the waterwheels and shafts of the textile mills.

On the outskirts of Bingley stands one of the finest, and certainly the most unique, structures to be found on the Leeds and Liverpool Canal. Bingley Five Rise Locks represent a notable feat of civil engineering, which, together with the nearby Three Rise Locks, raises the canal ninety feet. It resembles a giant staircase, which is what it basically is. The five integral locks raise, or lower, craft through a series of deep chambers, separated by massive oak gates. Stand beside Top Lock and look down. The full impact of the canal's dramatic fall is clearly demonstrated and an extensive view of Bingley and the Aire valley unfurls beneath you. A tribute to the skill and dedication of its stonemasons and carpenters, the locks have been superbly maintained for over 220 years. A plaque on the wall of Top Lock House displays the names of the four stonemasons responsible for its construction.

At this point, what is probably the most popular section of the Leeds and Liverpool Canal, begins. There are seventeen miles of unrestricted passage until the five locks at Gargrave are encountered, making it ideal for today's pleasure craft. This flat and fertile valley is a typical West Riding blend of industry and engaging panoramas. The canal alternately passes between green pastureland, flanked by rolling hills, and former mill settlements, some of which still cling tentatively to their textile heritage.

The River Aire is still a close companion as the canal sets a course for Keighley, the next sizeable township. As it passes beneath the attractive hamlet of Micklethwaite, it is spanned by another swing bridge that causes consternation for motorists using the narrow road that it serves. A collection of well-groomed stone cottages set into the

Canalmen pose during repairs to Bingley Five Rise Locks in 1909

hillside, Micklethwaite offers unrivalled views across the broad valley, to where the wooded Bingley St. Ive's estate and the rock formation of Druid's Altar stand aloof. Above Micklethwaite the slopes clamber up to the heights of Rombald's Moor, that separates the valley from Wharfedale.

Pleasant footpaths radiate from the canal hereabouts to criss-cross the surrounding fields and high meadows. These offer a selection of stimulating walks and the opportunity to explore the settlements of East Morton and Riddlesden.

In the valley bottom, on the fringe of Riddlesden and Keighley, sit the remains of East Riddlesden Hall, a historic building that stands on the site of a former grange for Bolton Priory. Sandwiched between canal and river it was rebuilt in 1640 for James Murgatroyd, a Halifax clothier. The Murgatroyd family gained a notorious reputation and some of them were imprisoned by the state. The church declared them excommunicate for their excesses and profanity.

The tranquil pond, which welcomes visitors when they enter the grounds, was originally fished by the monks of Bolton Priory. Nearby stands a medieval Tithe Barn, now carefully restored and housing a collection of farm carts and implements. There is a gift shop and tearoom on site and a tour of the hall is available. If you

Horse-drawn canal barge

opt for the tour, beware of the ghost that allegedly looks out of the 'Catherine Wheel' window above the two-storey porch.

Down to earth Keighley is a settlement of long standing, but it became a town a little more than 200 years ago. The textile expansion at that time led to a quick rise in population, as it did in many local villages. Keighley was at the forefront of textile manufacture, which has contracted and is now supplemented by engineering and other industries. Although the Leeds and Liverpool Canal skirts the northern edge of the town, it was highly instrumental in its industrial growth.

The town stands at the base of the Worth Valley, close to the point where the River Worth joins forces with the River Aire. It is well known as the starting point of the Worth Valley Railway, immortalised in the film *The Railway Children*. Countless youngsters have enjoyed a thrilling steam journey through Brontë country to Haworth and Oxenhope.

The brooding hills that protect the town display the wild landscapes depicted in the Brontë novels, particularly the windswept moorland setting of Top Withens. Keighley itself possesses many fine Victorian buildings, including Cliffe Castle, which is situated in appealing grounds. The former home of rich mill owners, its mid-Victorian design incorporates Italianate features. In 1950, it was donated to the town by Sir Bracewell Smith and it has proved to be a very popular gift. People flock to its parkland, gardens and aviary, in addition to the house itself, which contains an admirable museum. Amongst its displays is the last handloom used in Airedale by Timothy ('Timmy') Feather, of Stanbury, near Haworth.

Another tempting stretch of Airedale beckons beyond Keighley, as the canal journeys towards Skipton in the shadow of industrial villages, such as Silsden, Steeton, Cross Hills and Glusburn. The legacy of the textile industry is recalled by another prominent chimney bearing the word 'Damart', which belongs to one of the few remaining mills in the area.

At Kildwick, within sight of another eye-catching stone bridge, the tower of St. Andrew's Parish Church protrudes over a high canalside wall, as if anxious not to be missed. It certainly should not be, for it is a fine building, which is sometimes described as the 'Lang Kirk O' Craven.' This is an apt description, for it is 170 feet long and its extended knave is one of the longest in Yorkshire. Some of its interesting features include fragments of a Saxon Cross, and a decorative doorway that is topped by a seventeenth-century sundial. One of the pews, used by a local family, carries the inscription 'EE 1633,' a reference to Edward Eltoft, Lord of the Manor of Farnhill.

Kildwick Hall, the former residence of the local gentry, still remains on the outskirts of the village, a fine Jacobean building that has been converted into a hotel. The church occupies a prominent position above the meandering River Aire, in close proximity to the White Lion, an inn of character. Situated below these landmarks, sturdy Kildwick Bridge now enjoys an easier life. It formerly carried the old main road to Skipton, which has been replaced by the modern Aire Valley Trunk Road, across the river. Traffic now rushes through the valley bottom and is kept at arm's length from Kildwick and its neighbour, Farnhill. These settlements nestle beneath Farnhill Moor, which is ablaze with purple heather in late summer. Balancing on its rim is the prominent cross, known as Farnhill Pinnacle, its unusual cement-rendered base, creating an unconventional spectacle. At the foot of the pinnacle lies a large weathered stone bearing an inscription commemorating Queen Victoria's golden jubilee in 1897.

The canal enjoys an elevated ride on an embankment as it flows through Farnhill, permitting commendable views over the valley and the snaking River Aire. From the angular slopes of Low Bradley

Moor a glimpse of the distant hills of the Yorkshire Dales can be obtained, their hazy outlines beckoning beyond Skipton, the market town known as the 'Gateway to the Dales.' Not only is it a busy tourist centre, it has a thriving industrial base, demonstrated by the array of warehouses and factories that guard its entrance. Its beginnings were based on agriculture and it was the possessor of a great corn market before the influx of textile mills. Skipton has long been an important centre for the auction of livestock and it is a rich mixture of past and present. A restored thirteenth-century corn mill can be found on the banks of the Eller Beck, utilising two waterwheels harnessed to millstones and a further one to power agricultural machinery.

Skipton is normally thronged with visitors, bustling around its market stalls on the cobbles of the High Street, or pouring into its wide assortment of shops. There are many other attractions to this eminent Dales town and two of them occupy pride of place at the head of the High Street. The stately castle presides over a protective garland of trees that mask its entrance and in close proximity stands Holy Trinity Church. Both of these buildings have an extensive history, stretching back to the time of William the Conqueror. Robert de Romille created a Norman stronghold, probably a wooden structure on an earth mound, after his receipt of the Honour of Skipton from William, but the de Romille tenure was to prove a brief one. The most successful occupants of the defensive site were the Cliffords, later to become the Earls of Cumberland, who held the castle and its estates from 1311 until the death of Lady Anne Clifford, the last of the line, in 1676. It was this redoubtable lady who restored the castle and the church following their damage during the Civil War. She repaired the ravages wrought by Cromwell's siege of the castle and rebuilt the gatehouse, on whose parapet can be seen the family motto 'Desormais,' meaning henceforth.

Lady Anne, a remarkable character, also left her imprint on the Yorkshire Dales, for since the Dissolution of the Monasteries, the Cliffords had owned a large portion of them. She established an historic 'trail' that traversed the valleys of the Wharfe, Ure, Lune and Eden to her castle at Brougham. She frequently travelled this route restoring the properties that she owned, which included the castles of Pendragon, Appleby and Brougham. Since her valiant efforts, no one has taken up the challenge and many of these historic buildings have fallen into decay.

Amongst the Clifford memorials in the adjacent church is the magnificent table-tomb, bearing heraldic shields, which Lady Anne erected in memory of her father. This place of worship, constructed in the traditional Perpendicular style of the Craven district, possesses an impressive tower that dominates the head of the High Street. I was lucky enough to be given a tour of this edifice that culminated in an excellent 'birds-eye' view of the town from its battlements. The view was captivating until I suffered the sensation that the buildings within my gaze were swaying. I was not comforted to learn that it was in fact me who was gently moving, rather than the town. There was a high wind at the time and the tower, I discovered, was designed to flex in order to prevent structural damage.

The Craven Museum is located near the castle and it contains a variety of exhibits concerning the life and history of the locality. Of particular note are collections of historical artefacts, geological specimens and tools that were used in the local industries of lead mining and quarrying.

Skipton is a very popular mooring place on the Leeds and Liverpool Canal and no spot is more in demand than the Springs Branch, a disused cul-de-sac that was constructed in 1797 to serve the stone quarry situated near the castle. It begins at the foot of a limestone precipice and travels for less than one quarter of a mile to join the main canal at the decorative Watermill Bridge. Stroll along its towpath on a summer's day and you will find an array of craft hugging its moorings amongst pleasant tree-lined surroundings.

It is hard to bid farewell to Skipton, but river and canal lead out of town and into the Craven countryside that separates it from Gargrave. The two watercourses keep in close harmony as they weave through a valley that once contained a post-glacial lake. As they pass under the busy Skipton by-pass they enter tranquil surroundings, where sunshine adds lustre to a fresh and green landscape. In such conditions I have seen the waters of the canal turn a startling blue, their reflective surface resembling a canvas of shimmering white, azure and emerald.

In my view, this is an ideal setting for the quiet and contemplative pastime of fishing. I do not know if many of the perch, tench and bream, that inhabit the canal, can be found here, but it is certainly an attractive part of the canal to fish. The peaceful vicinity is immune from the noise and disturbance of habitation that distracts fishermen and, more importantly, the fish themselves. I understand that the fisherman's worst enemies are thoughtless children and even more thoughtless adults, who enjoy hurling missiles into the canal, which range from small stones to sizeable chunks of wood and rock.

Set in this fertile landscape of woods and parkland, lies Gargrave, three miles beyond Skipton, and our last port of call on the Leeds and Liverpool Canal. The village is encircled by engaging hills and exudes a quiet and unhurried charm. It marks the entrance to Malhamdale and has the distinction of providing a halt on the Pennine Way.

Many motorists hurry through, antennae trained on Settle or Lakeland, but Gargrave deserves better than the cursory glance. In monastic times it had connections with Sawley Abbey, in Ribblesdale, and the parish church has a long history that emanates from the Anglo Danish era. There are crosses in its north porch that date from this period. The village is an ideal centre for walkers, surrounded as it is by winding lanes and rambling footpaths. It makes a small concession to industry, which is demonstrated by the Johnson and Johnson surgical dressing factory.

In the centre of the village, the Aire is straddled by a splendid three-arched bridge, built of warm local stone. It carries Pennine Way walkers over the river and introduces them to the nearby Dalesman Café, a mecca for cyclists and walkers. Here they can relax, re-fuel and have a natter with like-minded enthusiasts. To those walking north on the Pennine Way, it offers the opportunity to savour the forthcoming section of their ordeal, which passes through the admirable limestone countryside of Malhamdale.

The popular long-distance footpath crosses the canal, by means of a stone bridge, as it leaves Gargrave and heads north to Eshton Moor and thereafter to join forces with the infant River Aire. From the bridge we will say goodbye to the Leeds and Liverpool Canal as we look down on the first series of locks encountered since leaving Bingley.

The canal continues westwards to carry on its climb into the high Pennines, where, even when traffic was at its height, only about ten percent passed through on the way to the cotton towns of Lancashire.

Winter at Tan Hill

CHAPTER FIVE

The Roving Reporter

Ice-cold, relentless waves lapped terrifyingly close to the abandoned reporter as the helicopter shrank to a mere speck on the horizon. He stood transfixed by the realisation that he was completely marooned on the shifting strands of the Goodwin Sands. The thought of 30,000 sailors and their vessels that had perished in the vice-like grip of the treacherous quick sands on which he was standing did nothing to allay his fear. Panic mounted as he brooded upon the frailty of the disappearing helicopter. This should not have happened, he told himself, as he silently cursed his over-enthusiastic director.

The hapless reporter was in the process of presenting an episode of *Remote Britain,* a series being filmed for BBC Television. In order to illustrate the dangers of the quick sands, the director had hit upon the idea of filming his front man becoming stranded by the swiftly rising tide. He had been full of assurances that the helicopter, carrying the camera-crew, would return quickly to pick up the reporter. Unfortunately, as the helicopter flew away, camera running, the director over-enthusiastically ordered the pilot to get farther out of range of its unfortunate subject than had been mooted. As the tiny figure on the sands disappeared, the director rubbed his hands in delight at the resulting effect and reneged on his promise to return immediately for the marooned protagonist.

Scanning the empty sky, the reporter grappled with terrifying thoughts such as what would happen if the helicopter's engine failed, but fortunately, all ended well. The helicopter returned to snatch the castaway from the sands as the water encircled his feet. His remarks to the errant director are not recorded.

If that alarming episode had ended tragically, we would have lost the opportunity to enjoy one of the most successful television series of recent years, for the reporter involved is Luke Casey, originator and linchpin of the *Dales Diary.* Luke, who possesses a warm sense of humour, is now able to laugh at his predicament on that daunting day.

Born in Ireland, he has, I am sure, earned the title of honorary

Harvest time at Keld

Yorkshireman for bringing the beauty of the county, and particularly the Dales, into thousands of homes. Luke attributes his love of the countryside to his birthplace on the shores of Loch Conn in County Mayo, which he describes as a beguiling area of hills and lakes. Raised amongst the indigenous farming communities, he experienced a very similar way of life to that of the Dales. Animals, naturally, have played a large role in his life. Over the years he has kept ponies, pigs, and hens, substantially for his children's enjoyment, and has also indulged his passion for dogs. He is particularly fond of Labradors, which he bred at one time, and currently owns one called Murphy, named after the Irish stout.

Luke's first assignment was as junior reporter on the Northern Echo, based in Darlington. It was during the 1960's, and he had left his native Ireland for a life of newsgathering in the north east of England. His particular patch covered part of the North York Moors, where as District Reporter, he was required to roam the former iron-

Aysgarth Falls

mining area that includes Guisborough and neighbouring villages. He tackled his fledgling career with gusto, revelling in his access to the heather-clad moorland and picturesque villages of the Cleveland Hills. He found that his beat provided the perfect introduction to the Yorkshire countryside.

Luke became acquainted with the Yorkshire Dales through John North, a local newspaper columnist, who compiled regular pieces concerning the area in a *Down Your Way* style series. In his spare time Luke explored many of the places featured in the articles and discovered not only their intrinsic beauty, but also the indomitable spirit of dalesfolk. He quickly developed the profound empathy with the Dales and its inhabitants that he portrays so effectively on the *Dales Diary.*

An even greater opportunity to scrutinise the Dales arose when he joined the BBC in Newcastle as an outside broadcaster with the *Look North* team. The programme covered Teesside, his home ground, the North York Moors and the Dales. By this time Luke's job had also become his hobby and he grasped every opportunity to discover more about the areas that he visited during filming.

Eventually he gravitated to London and worked for the BBC's

Nationwide for several years. At that time the programme was fronted by such household names as Michael Barrett and Sue Lawley. Luke continued to indulge his interest in the outdoors as a roving reporter and a catalogue of stimulating assignments ensued. Some of these provided more excitement than he had anticipated, including the one concerning the Goodwin Sands. That particular series, *Remote Britain*, featured other diverse locations such as a canal in Ireland and remote Rockall in the North Atlantic.

In the episode concerning the Irish canal, which incidentally lies in his home county of Mayo, he related a tale of disaster. The Cong Canal was constructed during the potato famine of the mid-nineteenth century and formed one of many projects designed to provide work during a period of mass unemployment. The intention was to link two lochs, Corrib and Mask, that are divided by a strip of land intriguingly named 'Joyce's Country.' The canal, named after the town of Cong, which lies on the border between Mayo and Galway, developed into a fiasco. On its completion the water refused to flow due to a misjudgment regarding the gradient. In his report on the sorry incident Luke was relieved to point out that the designer was an Englishman.

His mission to Rockall, the rocky bastion lying to the west of the Outer Hebrides, involved a voyage of 200 miles. Jutting from surrounding fishing grounds its name is familiar to all those who listen to the shipping forecast on the radio. It forms the highest point of a great submarine bank, which was annexed by Britain in 1955. As the film crew approached the rock, someone had the bright idea of planting a *Nationwide* flag on it, which proved no easy task. Luke unfortunately fell into the sea during his attempt to clamber onto its daunting crags and the flag was eventually put in place by a nimble member of the crew.

One of his most interesting assignments of *Remote Britain* involved a cattle-drove through the Scottish Highlands in 1981. This re-enactment began on the Isle of Skye and followed a genuine drove route to the former Tryst at Crieff in Perthshire. It was organised and led by John Keay whose intention was to travel and live as the original drovers had, utilising ponies and sleeping under canvas, or in bothies.

Remote Britain featured the group's progress, which involved Luke and the film crew travelling with the modern-day drovers and periodically departing to put an episode together. It proved to be an inspiring and unforgettable experience and provided a rare insight into the hardships endured during those austere times. Luke was struck by the wild beauty of the remote glens and awesome mountains that were encountered and also by the tenacity of the drovers.

The complete journey took two months and John Keay wrote an account of the experience in *Highland Drove*, which proved a worthy sequel to his works on India and on Himalayan exploration. The route that he describes is shown in the maps that are included in this chapter.

The idea germinated whilst John was studying the Highland droving tradition and he, along with his wife Julia, attempted to recreate one of the most arduous and dramatic of all Scottish droves. With assorted friends, dogs and ponies, they planned to set off from the west coast of Skye and drive a herd of Highland cattle over 200 testing miles to Crieff.

The drove itself, however, proved not the most difficult part of the project. Initially they had to run the gauntlet of wise sages who declared that such a task was impossible. These included farmers, lairds, factors and stockmen who said 'they'll just lie down and die', implying modern cattle would be too heavy to survive the rigours of such a journey. These constant discouragements only served to strengthen John's resolve.

The next major obstacle was the acquisition of thirty head of cattle. Following many disappointments, help came from an unexpected source; the laird of Barrisdale, who provided seventeen bullocks. This slice of luck seemed to act as a spur and offers of further cattle gathered momentum. A full complement was soon mustered; a motley mixture of shaggy beasts that ranged from the gentle, that seemed embarrassed by their large, preposterous horns, to the fearful, that would shy at the slightest provocation and run away from the smallest obstacle. It became abundantly clear that the biggest challenge would be handling the cattle. The realisation dawned that it was not so much a question of reaching Crieff, as one of containing unruly cattle in the wild, open country that awaited them on the opening leg of the journey, from Drynoch to Sligachan. The team embarked on a crash course in cattle handling, in an effort to acquire some expertise.

At last they set off on a bright October morning, ponies champing at the bit and knee-deep in collies. They threaded through

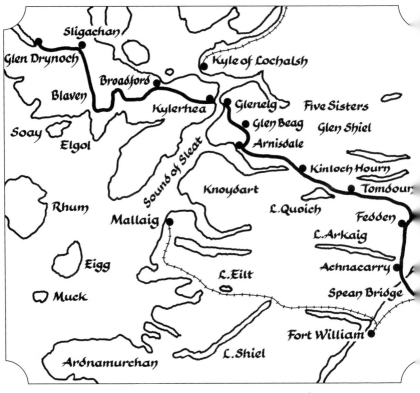

Highland Drove – Skye to Spean Bridge

the mighty Cuillins by way of Glen Sligachan, in order to keep away from the road and to gain valuable experience in controlling beasts in secluded country. At their first water crossing, ponies floundered and dogs splashed, but the beasts waded confidently across. The first obstacle of a journey that would include crossing swollen rivers, climbing rocky gradients and combating appalling weather, had, much to their relief, been overcome. They snaked a circuitous path to Broadford and a subsequent climb through Glen Arroch took them to a watershed that permits fine views of Broadford Bay with the Skye hills beyond and of the hills of Glenelg across the Sound of Sleat.

The crossing of this narrow and turbulent strip of water, that separates Kylerhea from the mainland, formed their next challenge and, for authenticity, it was planned to swim the cattle across. Originally the beasts were roped together for this manoeuvre, one end of the rope passing round the under jaw of an animal and the other

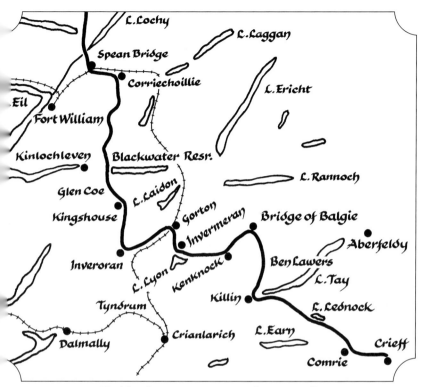

Highland Drove – Spean Bridge to Crieff

end tied to the tail of the one in front. A man in the stern of a boat would pull along a string of six to eight animals by holding the rope of the foremost one.

This system has its dangers and for safety reasons the cattle were taken across by ferry. It was a wise move for the swift currents of the Sound of Sleat threaten to sweep away any that are poorly secured. In former times, piers were primitive and methods of landing cattle from boats were rough. Most animals were forced overboard into the water, but sometimes a simple block and tackle was used to hoist them out of larger boats. Fortunately for John and his team no such problems exist today.

After a trouble-free crossing it was time to head into the mainland mountains and follow a course that was surveyed as long ago as 1804, during the road-building era, by Thomas Telford. Despite his efforts, parts of the route remain un-metalled. It skirts quiet Loch Hourn and the lonely peninsular of Knoydart. In the time of the drovers it offered substantial upland pasture and secluded overnight resting-places. Typical of many such tracks through inhospitable countryside, it had been pioneered by the early cattle-raiders, a thriving occupation for several hundred years.

Arnisdale and Kinloch Hourn were two resting-places used by John and his band before reaching Loch Quoich and entering Glen Garry. Having achieved some semblance of handling their charges, they ceased to panic if any cattle strayed overnight. To recover them, they simply followed the trail of cowpats the following morning!

The former drovers' inn at Tomdoun provided a rewarding halt whilst negotiating the narrow road that hugs the shore of Loch Garry. Known as 'Telford's road', it once formed part of the old Road to the Isles, which turned north at Tomdoun. At the inn the perspiring party slaked their thirst, savoring their first alcoholic drink for four days.

Their contentment was soon shattered by the discovery that the hooves of the cattle were suffering from wear due to the hard ground. This disaster was compounded by their horns, which had gone floppy. Desperately John searched for a remedy and eventually it was realised that the two maladies could have a common cause – calcium deficiency. The problem was finally traced to an overdose of magnesium that was present in the cattle cobs that supplemented the animals' diet of herbage. The sponsors, who had supplied the offending cobs, immediately arranged to deliver a fresh consignment and an intermediate remedy was also undertaken. The cattle were given a primitive foot bath, utilsing a disused fish tank. Thereafter, twenty gallons of evil-smelling solution were humped by the party in order that the performance could be repeated at intervals.

Near the head of Loch Garry the drove-route swings south and here the cattle at one time either forded the River Garry, or swam across the narrow head of the loch. There is now a bridge at the point where the loch narrows and a slender road leads from it to the former stance, or resting-place, at Greenfield. Here, they rested overnight before the climb to another watershed and the ruined bothy at Fedden, tucked away amongst the hills of Lochaber.

There followed a long descent through the defile of Gleann Cia-aig, which brought them to the 'Dark Mile' that lies at the eastern end of Glen Arkaig. It is so named because the road into the glen tunnels through a dark avenue of trees. The area was immortalised by D.K. Broster in her trilogy of novels that are based upon the 1745

Luke amidst the limestone of the Yorkshire Dales

The Swale Gorge from Kisdon Hill

Langthwaite, Arkengarthdale

Coverham Abbey entrance and farm, Coverdale

Jacobite rebellion.

Now within spitting distance of the watery gash that splits the Highlands, the Great Glen, another dilemma had to be overcome. This was how to get the cattle safely over the busy arterial road that courses through the glen. The solution, to which there seemed no alternative, was to ferry them across in a cattle transporter and the beasts appeared to appreciate the unexpected lift.

Their next objective, Spean Bridge, was recognised as a key point for traffic passing at the west end of the Great Glen as long ago as the Jacobite uprisings and it was here that General Wade built the High Bridge of Spean in 1723. The general was responsible for the construction of military roads through the Highlands during this troublesome period.

Here, in the shadow of the Ben Nevis mountain range, they climbed to another bothy, set deep in Lairig Leacach, a narrow defile that skirts the eastern edge of the Grey Corries, a spur of ridges and peaks radiating from Ben Nevis itself and Aonach Beag. Under heavy cloud and persistent rain, they followed this deep channel through majestic mountains until, in clearer weather, they were able to progress to Loch Eilde Beag, where a night's rest awaited them.

Bleak moorland confronted the battle-hardened travellers on the following day during their trek to the lonely Blackwater Reservoir and uppermost in their minds was the daunting prospect of Rannoch Moor, one of the most exposed and desolate tracts of country in Britain. This nagging fear had to be put on the back burner, however, whilst they tussled with a new enemy, deep, clingy peat, that nearly marooned the ponies as they headed for the reservoir. Mercifully, the cattle seemed untroubled by the treacherous terrain and trotted happily along. The ponies proved a much greater problem and they were lucky to reach the reservoir without breaking a leg.

That evening the party sat, under a canopy of twinkling stars, round a roaring fire and relaxed for what was probably the first time during their journey. Full of bravado the following morning they took the direct route, over open country to Kingshouse, scorning the glen through to Altnafeadh and a section of road. Some hours later they crested the ridge that overlooks the Kingshouse Hotel and drank in the awesome splendour of the Moor of Rannoch. In this great wilderness, the hotel is a positive oasis and it provides an excellent staging post on the West Highland Way that crosses the moor. This I can vouch for, having spent a memorable night there whilst walking

Scotland's first officially designated long-distance footpath, that runs from the outskirts of Glasgow to Fort William.

Their stance that night was adjacent to Blackrock Cottage, a climbing hut belonging to the Ladies' Scottish Climbing Club, tucked away amongst the heather not far from the hotel. Despite their blossoming confidence, born of the accomplishment of the larger part of their journey, the forthcoming crossing of Rannoch Moor still rang alarm bells in their sub-conscious. Most of the team was awake early on the following morning, wondering what the day had in store.

Their worries proved to be unfounded, for, in reasonable weather conditions, they were able to cross the moor, by way of one of Wade's military roads, albeit still a rough track, without incident.

Floppy horns and sore feet were now under control, thanks to a change of diet and frequent foot baths.

Luke was fortunately accompanying the drove at this particular stage and he considers it one of the highlights of the project. He will always remember the eight miles of desolate moorland that they traversed that day culminating in their arrival at Black Mount on the shore of the idyllic Loch Tulla, which lies near Bridge of Orchy. Another memory of that inspiring day concerns the poor film crew who had to lug their equipment over the wild moor.

That evening the drovers enjoyed a celebratory ceilidh, organised by friends, that added spice to their sparse social lives. They were able to forget, for a brief period, the trials and hardships of a repetitive daily routine.

The next day saw them heading east along the fringe of Loch Tulla to another bothy at Gorton, near Achallader. At this point they were searching for the best route through the mountains that encircle the head of Glen Lyon. They decided upon secluded Glen Meran that squeezes through a narrow gap between Ben a' Chreachain and Meall Bhuide to enter one of Scotland's loveliest and most inaccessible glens. John discovered that this route had, at one time, not only been used by drovers, but also by cattle thieves smuggling their booty from the lowlands onto Rannoch Moor.

Their entry into the wild upland wastes of Glen Lyon was heralded by a finger of water that did not exist prior to Loch Lyon's conversion into a reservoir. When the mighty dam was constructed at its eastern end the loch's size increased threefold, drowning the tiny settlement of Invermeran.

The team was forced to edge their way around this swollen water-source along several miles of rough hillsides before entering the scenic corridor that leads to Bridge of Balgie, their next destination. When it reached this scattering of buildings, secreted in the heart of Glen Lyon, another steep and twisting climb presented itself. This provided a stiff test of stamina, but the cattle, now well acclimatised to demanding gradients, seemed, despite their sore feet, fitter and more resolute than at any previous stage of their ordeal. They walked, heads lowered against driving hail, forelocks windswept and their great horns, not so floppy now, gently undulating.

Beasts and drovers crested the watershed that lies in the shadow of Ben Lawers, the highest mountain in Perthshire, sensing that success was now within reach. The weather-beaten band had only to negotiate the steep hillsides that rake down to the shore of Loch Tay, to be within easy reach of Killin, their next stance.

In contrast to the encouraging state of the animals, the drovers were beginning to wilt and even the foaming display of the Falls of Dochart, failed to lift them from their lethargy on their arrival in the popular holiday village. Things improved, however, during their overnight rest in Killin, for thanks to Luke and the *Nationwide* team, plus other members of the media, the fame of the drove was spreading and an enthusiastic welcome awaited the jaded drovers in the pub that evening when drinks were on the house.

Upon their departure the following morning they were accompanied by a large crowd to the outskirts of the village, where the final twenty miles of their ordeal began. These were completed in a heady trance, humans and beasts entangled in a monotonous routine. Through the hills on the south side of Loch Tay they plodded, passing Lochan Breaclaich and forging towards Glen Lednock, minds barely focusing on anything other than the repetitive movement of the herd. At ten o'clock that evening, after many exhausting hours on the march, the weary party tumbled into their tents perched on the hills above Comrie. As they drifted into slumber their thoughts were on the final few miles of their ordeal. Could it all be really coming to an end in less than twenty-four hours?

Next morning, at first light, the cattle, which were the real winners in the whole charade, simply filed out of the field without any urging and began to stroll down the glen. They were now dictating the pace and they had succeeded in reducing the drovers to

Middleham Cross and Castle

their unhurried tempo. However, for the rest of the day, the cattle acquitted themselves admirably, neither straying from the group, nor frightening the many onlookers who lined the streets of Comrie to welcome them.

Leaving the well-wishers cheering in their wake, the drove ambled through Strathearn, bathed in sunshine; fitting conditions for the completion of their journey. On the outskirts of Crieff they halted and rested overnight, planning to cover the last mile to the town centre on the following morning.

This they did, to a rousing reception. A police escort, pipers and the television crew accompanied the victorious team through cheering crowds to journey's end.

Suddenly, it was all over. The enthusiastic crowds were no more and two months of struggle and privation that had forged a firm bond between drovers and beasts would soon fade into memory. All is not forgotten, however, for recollections of that pioneering challenge will always remain with Luke, who feels privileged to have accompanied John and his team on a great adventure.

Luke's family remained in the North East during his period with *Nationwide.* The decision not to relocate was made on account of their children - two sons and three daughters. His dislike of London, which he found claustrophobic, as he does most towns and cities, ensured that they would be raised in the North, which he feels has

Sutton Bank – near the Hambleton Drove Road

integrity and spaciousness.

This proved to be a wise choice, for Luke was soon travelling the world as one of three reporters in the BBC's *Money Programme* team. For roughly four years he featured on many international assignments, ranging from the future of Hong Kong to the horse-racing industry in Kentucky and Maryland. It was whilst reporting on the latter that he was able to indulge his love of horses, indicative of his Irish blood. The feature gave an insight into the vast amounts of money involved in the breeding of racehorses. He was privileged to meet 'Northern Dancer', the legendary stallion that earned $30,000,000 during one year of semi-retirement, for nomination to mares. To you and me that means receiving a fantastic sum of money, despite fading powers, for fathering some of the greatest horses in racing history. His first famous son was 'Nijinski', the Derby winner sired for Vincent O'Brien. This gifted trainer had recognised the stallion's remarkable qualities and he sent an appropriate mare to Northern Dancer's stud. Since that time, the great money-earner, which can literally be described as the 'daddy of them all' has produced many other famous offspring.

Despite the exciting nature of his globe-trotting lifestyle, Luke decided to return home and spend more time with his family. Although his itinerant wanderings are now confined to Yorkshire and the North East, he is content to devote his energies to these areas, for which he holds the greatest affection.

Luke transferred to Tyne Tees Television, as it was known at that time. He has continued his fulfilling career during a period of change within the industry, for the company is now part of Granada / Tyne Tees / Yorkshire Television.

Fate took a hand shortly after his return to the North East when a former colleague from *Nationwide,* who had become Managing Director of Zenith North, a television production company, suggested a series of outside broadcasts covering the Yorkshire Dales. This was a wonderful opportunity for Luke, who grabbed it with both hands. From that idea grew the *Dales Diary,* that is now in its seventh year. During the life of the programme Luke has become a familiar face on our television screens, exuding an enthusiasm for all aspects of the Dales, particularly its people. His greatest satisfaction is that dalesfolk love the programme, which is due in no small measure to his maxim that they should be portrayed exactly as they are and not patronised. He considers them to be extraordinary people and his respect and admiration is distinctly evident during his interviews.

Luke talks passionately about the Dales, which he finds inspirational. Their greatest attribute, he believes, is the provision of continuity amidst changing times. In its folds he enjoys the rejuvenating forces of peace and solitude, but laments the exodus of people following the demise of the lead-mining and knitting industries. One encouraging trend that Luke has discovered shows that increasing numbers of expatriate dalesfolk are returning to their native surroundings after raising families elsewhere.

The indispensable qualities possessed by the hardy communities that still inhabit the more remote dales, are, he feels, stoicism and adaptability. Despite their isolation, Luke senses a genuine thirst for knowledge. Many of the older people, he finds, are self-taught and possess an inbred intelligence, which belies their simple lifestyle. Artistic traits also manifest themselves through poetry and painting, which, he contends, are inspired by the enduring appeal of their locality.

Yorkshire and its Dales possess, of course, an ample share of 'characters' and the *Dales Diary* has featured many of these during its life span. Two of the most memorable that Luke has encountered are a Swaledale farmer and an octogenarian cyclist. The former, Jim Alderson, an 'up-dale' farmer, in his seventies, hails from Keld, the delightful hamlet that straddles the infant River Swale. Luke relished the opportunity of interviewing Jim, whom he describes as a 'true dalesman', in what is one of his own favourite locations.

He was filmed herding his sheep in the wilds of upper Swaledale, just as his family had done for generations. Jim told the viewers that both he and his wife were baptised in the Swale, which he refers to as the 'Jordan of England'. The more he talked, according to Luke, the affection he held for his 'home' dale, his farm and his flock became abundantly clear. Tales of rescuing and nurturing his lambs brought a tear to his eye and Luke realised that beneath that rough persona lay an innate tenderness. This was borne out by Jim's admission that he never failed to get a thrill every time he saw a newborn lamb.

Another revelation by Jim concerned the former Cathole Inn; he was responsible for its demise! The inn was offered for sale in 1965 and Jim bought it. He converted it into a dwelling, thus rendering Keld a 'dry' village. Many thirsty walkers tramp through, or stay overnight, in the village, which conveniently stands at the junction of the Pennine Way and Wainwright's Coast to Coast footpaths. They would be hard put to find a drink in the locality, if it were not one of the facilities available at East Stonesdale farm. This well-patronised B and B, run by Ernest and Doreen Whitehead is known to many a weary traveller and the ebullient Mrs. Whitehead has compiled a *Coast to Coast Bed and Breakfast Accommodation Guide*. The friendly couple are well known to Jim and they share a profound respect for their neighbourhood and its inhabitants.

The cyclist, Donald 'Gig' Lee, was eighty-seven at the time of his appearance on the *Dales Diary*. Throughout his extensive life he had cycled in the Dales and he was able to highlight many changes that had taken place within his memory. A life-long member of the Cyclists' Touring Club, he had gravitated to its senior section, the Autumn Tints. He recalled bygone excursions into the Dales when there was a welcome at almost every farmhouse. At that time farmers' wives provided high teas for cyclists and walkers, in order to encourage visitors.

In Luke's opinion, Donald epitomized the original Dales tourist, who had earned the right to travel within them at will, whilst indulging his passion for dalesfolk and their environment. Donald thought nothing of covering up to 140 miles per day, in all weathers, safe in the knowledge that he would be welcomed wherever he travelled. He bemoaned some of the changes that have occurred over the years, indicating that he finds the modern cafés too expensive and is reduced to carrying his own food and a flask.

Time appeared to have untouched this unique character, which eschewed the multi-coloured Lycra gear and lightweight bikes of today. He turned up for filming on the ancient, heavy 'boneshaker' that he still rode. The director explained to Donald that he wished to take a shot of him appearing from a distance and riding past the camera. He duly rode away, re-appearing at the appropriate moment. Unfortunately, it was not a sedate passage, for he flew past the camera and disappeared from view. Puzzled by this strange turn of events, one of the film-crew tried out his bike and to his horror discovered that it had no brakes!

Luke has illustrated the preferences of many of his subjects who have featured on the *Dales Diary*, but what about his own? Where are his favourite places? The area around Keld has already been mentioned and Wensleydale figures prominently in his affections. He considers this broad, lush valley to be 'England's green and pleasant land.' The beauty of this dale was portrayed in an episode which featured Freda White, affectionately known as 'Freda of Wenslydale', because of her ability to bring the past to life through her contributions to local dialect and folk songs. Luke is delighted to observe that the Wenslydale Creamery is currently flourishing, due in no small measure to its traditional Wensleydale cheese, made from the inimitable local milk. Quiet Coverdale and Arkengarthdale feature highly amongst his best-loved places, for their peace and solitude. The former he describes as the 'hidden dale', as it is tucked away amongst the furrows that flank Wensleydale. Not least among his favourites are Wharfedale and its upper branch, Langstrothdale, through which the infant River Wharfe playfully gurgles and cascades after beginning its life at Beckermonds.

His favourite places are not confined to the Dales, for Yorkshire has, of course, many other attributes. The western fringe of the North York Moors, around Osmotherly is one such location. He loves to walk the heather-clad moorland and ancient trackways that characterise the area. Perhaps his interest in drove-roads draws him to its centerpiece, the Hambleton Drove Road, which formed part of the route taken by Scottish drovers travelling to York and Malton. It lies on the line of a very old road that existed long before Roman times. Evidence of pre-historic man can still be found along its route, such as, Stone Age burial-mounds, earthworks and dykes. A section of the Cleveland Way, a popular National Trail, that covers the 110 miles between Helmsley and Filey, joins it for several miles.

The sole hostelry to survive from droving times is the Hambleton Hotel that lies on the A170, Thirsk to Scarborough road. There are several former drovers' inns within the vicinity, such as, Limekiln House, now a sad ruin, which formed the centre of the local lime burning and distribution trade. Chequers Farm, situated above Osmotherly, was formerly an excellent stance for Scottish cattle. The inn, as it was at that time, displayed a cryptic sign that welcomed travellers. It read 'Be not in haste   Step in and taste   Good ale for nothing – tomorrow!

Near to the Hambleton Hotel stands Dialstone House, which may have been a drovers' inn, but is better known for the 'dialstone', built into a roadside wall, which gives the house its name. It is claimed that on this stone stood the weighing machine for jockeys who rode at the once-famous Hambleton racecourse. Racehorses are apparently still exercised on the extensive stretches of turf just to the north of the Hambleton Hotel.

Osmotherly lies close to the start of a famous long-distance footpath that Luke featured in the *Dales Diary*. It is the Lyke Wake Walk, a test of endurance that stretches for forty miles to the North Sea at Ravenscar. The episode revealed that it was originated in 1955 by a local farmer, Bill Cowley, who's objective was to complete it within twenty-four hours. He successfully accomplished this and set a target that has become a part of long-distance walking legend. A couple who had walked the footpath whilst on their honeymoon, were also featured on the programme.

I am convinced that the *Dales Diary* will continue to provide a unique window on Dales life and culture for many years to come. Luke's close affinity with the area naturally produces certain aspirations for its future. Despite his optimism regarding the preservation of the locality's wellbeing, Luke's fervent hope is that a balance is maintained between farming and sporting interests. This, he contends, is of particular importance, in the light of the disappearance of thirty percent of Britain's heather-moorland since the Second World War. In his view, the trend of buying up hill-farms and their lands has to be carefully controlled; farmers must be allowed to keep their grazing rights, just as landowners must also be allowed to generate income through moorland management and the provision of sporting facilities.

A return to genuine tourism would be beneficial, in his opinion, to trades-people and farmers, who need the support and gratitude of visitors to the region. He feels that people should be encouraged to stay overnight, leave their cars and walk around. Exploration and greater contact with dalesfolk would, he maintains, go hand in hand with helping the local economy, by increased patronisation of local craft and souvenir shops, cafés and inns.

Luke regards the Dales as a 'living museum,' in which all should participate. He trusts that the Yorkshire Dales National Park Authority, that is responsible for the maintenance and administration of the greater part of the Dales, will continue to preserve the area in the best interests of its inhabitants and its traditions.

CHAPTER SIX

The Dales Way in Wharfedale

Compared to many other long-distance footpaths, the Dales Way is not particularly long or arduous, which is part of its appeal. It stretches for eighty-four miles from Ilkley to Bowness on Windermere and passes through scenery of the highest order. To aspiring long-distance walkers it offers the ideal initial challenge, for, as its name suggests, it primarily follows river valleys and involves a minimal amount of hill climbing.

The following account covers the initial portion of the footpath, which passes through Wharfedale, one of the most beautiful of the Yorkshire Dales. The River Wharfe, its name originates from the celtic 'swift water,' surges through the dale from its source at the tiny hamlet of Beckermonds to meet the River Ouse near Tadcaster. We join it at Ilkley and walk up-river for over thirty miles to its birthplace at the 'meeting of the two becks,' which gives Beckermonds its name.

The hallmark of the Dales Way is its great variety and Wharfedale contributes significantly in this respect. It offers unrivalled scenery, sweeping landscapes bounded by high fells and localities steeped in history and legend.

An auspicious start is provided by elegant Ilkley Old Bridge, with its rounded arches, which have spanned the Wharfe since the latter part of the seventeenth century. A fine example of a packhorse bridge, it replaced a series of wooden structures that were constantly damaged, or swept away, by the turbulent river. Wooden bridges had been utilised since the Middle Ages and, up to that era, the river had to be forded. During Roman times, when the site marked an important road intersection, it was one of the few places where the river could be crossed in relative safety.

On the nearby grassy mound that rises on the south side of the river and extends to the present Parish Church, stood the Roman fort of Olicana, a small garrison, built to guard the road junction. A visible reminder of the Roman occupation of Ilkley stands on top of the mound, in the form of a stone pillar, which marks the north

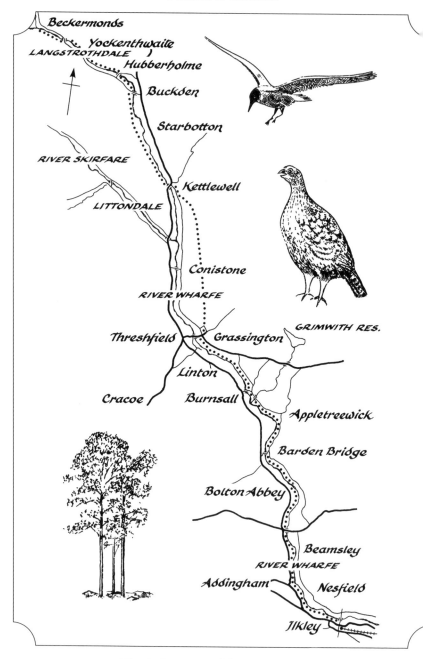

The Dales Way – Ilkley to Beckermonds

entrance to the fort.

The Parish Church houses two Roman altars beneath its west window, which have been modified to serve as the heads of windows. One of these exhibits the carving of a woman holding a torch in each hand and probably represents Demeter, the earth goddess. The other displays a carving of a pitcher and a flat dish with a handle, used for pouring barley into the sacred fire during sacrifices in Roman religious rites.

In the adjacent Manor House Museum, located within the sixteenth-century Manor House, are displayed interesting relics from the Roman era. Most prominent amongst these are two large, ornately-carved gravestones. Exhibits of course pottery, such as cooking-pots, dishes and a bowl used for grinding corn, are also featured, together with the elaborate base stone of a Roman Quern. Two stone heads, possibly representing gods, are a reminder of the religious superstitions of that age.

Ilkley has, of course, many other attractions. In addition to drawing multitudes of visitors each year to the White Wells bathhouse and the Cow and Calf rocks, the spa town is a magnet for walkers. Enter one of the many inviting cafés and you may trip over rucksacks of varying sizes. Mingle with the crowds jostling through the busy streets and you will find them purposefully striding the pavements, about to embark on one of the multitude of walks available in the locality. In addition to the Dales Way, there is its counterpart, the Ebor Way, which links Ilkley with York. Its name is derived from 'Eboracum,' the city's title in Roman times. If the thought of these two long-distant routes is daunting, there is a broad network of paths covering the surrounding area.

The initial stretch of the Dales Way rarely strays far from the riverbank, but there are many opportunities within the Wharfedale section for higher-level exploration. These are provided by numerous alternative paths that involve a little hill climbing, but provide the reward of extensive views of the valley.

The striking rural landscape of Wharfedale is soon revealed, as the path traverses rich pastureland that coats the wide valley. Luxuriant meadows are scattered with dark patterns of woodland and the high reaches of Ilkley Moor and Addingham Moorside dominate the view to the south. Across the grit stone edges of this wild upland ran a section of the important Bronze Age trade route, linking Ireland with the Continent. At various points along what was

The Church of Saint Peter, Addingham

the M62 motorway of its age, archeological evidence is visible of prehistoric man's passage, conveying tin, copper and gold. Stone circles, cup and ring stones and tumuli litter the moorland edge. One of the finest examples is the Swastika Stone, which bears an ornate carving that represents a Bronze Age symbol of eternal life.

To the north lies the dark mass of Blubberhouses Moor, a silent and remote area of heather and ling, disturbed only by the occasional intrepid walker and the cry of the curlew and the reclusive grouse.

Two miles from Ilkley, the river's flow is interrupted by a substantial weir, which formerly supplied power to the adjacent Low Mill, now a muted shell. The surrounding collection of renovated mill cottages is a joy to behold. Their immaculate facades are complemented by tiny, but colourful, gardens and every abode displays its name, each having an association with the redundant mill. 'Warp House', 'Weft Cottage' and 'The Shuttle' raise a smile from the passer-by.

A short walk along a narrow lane, within sight of the meandering Wharfe, brings into view the delightful grounds that surround the rectory adjacent to Addingham Parish Church. Resplendent, rolling

The chapel, Beamsley Hospital

lawns are cleaved by a tinkling brook and the plaintive call of peacocks, that inhabit the grounds, can often be heard.

Beyond the rectory the brook is crossed by means of a tiny stone bridge, which forms a fitting preview to the historic Church of St. Peter, standing amongst quiet meadows sprinkled with daffodil, or buttercup, according to the season. Although it is mainly of eighteenth-century construction, the present church retains numerous traces of the Tudor Period. During the reign of Henry VIII, a considerable amount of reconstruction was carried out by the local Vavasour family. The splendid knave roof is a fine example of their work, as are the chancel arch, aisle roof and windows in the north wall.

The church's early history can be traced to Norman times and beyond. Christians have worshipped at the site since the ninth century, and possibly earlier, for the Archbishop of York had a residence here in the eighth century. In 867, Archbishop Wulfhere took refuge in Addingham following the invasion of York by the Vikings and for eight years he led worship at a Saxon cross, part of which still remains in the current church. During those years,

Addingham was regarded as the ecclesiastical centre of the North and the resultant strengthening of the Christian community is commemorated by a group, currently attached to the church, known as the Wulfherans.

Another relic from the Viking period can be found on display on a pillar on the north side of the knave. It is a small comb case, made from bone, which was unearthed during excavation in the early 1970s.

The Way leaves this tranquil haven through a gap between a row of neat cottages that border the meadows. A dainty footbridge is crossed that squeezes between well-tended gardens, whose eye-catching colours add the final touch to this delightful corner of Addingham.

For those with time available, a slight detour is worthwhile to the notable main street of the village, which is thankfully free of heavy traffic since a by-pass was built a few years ago. Evidence can be seen of its industrial past and many of its stone buildings display a rich character.

The Wharfe is soon rejoined and the prominent cone of Beamsley Beacon fills the skyline to the east. This 1300 feet high landmark stands sentinel over the busy Skipton to Harrogate road and provides a natural barrier between Blubberhouses Moor and the rolling hills that surround Bolton Abbey. The eyes of the adventurous will be drawn to its craggy summit and the temptation to scale its beckoning slopes will be strong.

At the foot of the fell lies the hamlet of Beamsley, which has associations with Lady Anne Clifford, whose 'trail' is referred to in the chapter concerning the Leeds and Liverpool Canal. Her famous route, which began at Skipton Castle, entered Wharfedale near Beamsley and travelled up the dale as far as the village of Buckden. Consequently, there are two buildings in the dale which have her stamp upon them. The first of these is Beamsley Hospital, which comprises a unique round chapel and distinguished almshouses, that were completed by Lady Anne, following initial work by her mother. These dwellings were provided for poor widows of the period and they are still in use today.

As Bolton Bridge is approached, anyone prepared to climb to the viewpoint above Eller Carr Wood will be rewarded with one of the memorable vistas of Wharfedale. The features of the forthcoming section of the Dales Way are splendidly revealed within a panorama, whose centre-piece is the monastic ruin of Bolton Priory. In a

Ilkley Old Bridge

Bolton Priory

Kettlewell and Great Whernside

The River Wharfe near Starbotton

delightful riverside setting beyond stately Bolton Bridge, its remains lie beneath the impressive backdrop of distant Earl's Seat and Simon's Seat, the latter's grit stone summit once comprising a site of Druidical worship.

Closer inspection reveals that at Bolton Bridge there are, in fact, two bridges, a recent addition having been made to the original sturdy stone construction of 1673. The modern bridge is functional, rather than aesthetic, built to carry the demanding weight of modern traffic. It compares poorly to its worthy predecessor.

By way of compensation, the historic Devonshire Arms can be found nearby. Now an impressive hotel, it still bears the Coat of Arms of the Dukes of Devonshire, who have owned most of the estates between here and Barden Bridge, which stands several miles up-river, for many years.

At Bolton Bridge the Yorkshire Dales National Park is entered. It stretches for sixty miles to the north and encompasses a wide area. The continual aim of the National Park Authority, which is responsible for its administration, is to maintain its unspoiled beauty and the quality of life of its inhabitants.

From the bridge, the view up-river is enticing and a great affinity is felt with the river that hurries beneath your feet. Here, it flows freely, unfettered by the constrictions that lie in wait before it mingles with the waters of the North Sea. Bolton Priory, partially concealed by the curving riverbank, beckons from a distance, determined not to be overlooked.

The Dales Way has no such intention, for it passes within a stone's throw of its remains. All is not derelict at Bolton Priory because the knave of the Priory Church is intact and continues to be used as the Parish Church. A seventeenth-century building, which is now the rectory, shields the undamaged section of the monastic precincts from the eagerly approaching onlooker, but allows a clear view of the empty Decorated windows of the chancel and the remnants of the chapter house and living quarters. The melancholy beauty of this scene had a profound effect on the artist Turner, who painted many wonderful landscapes of the Yorkshire Dales.

Founded in 1697, at the bequest of Robert Boyle, the inventor of Boyle's Law, the Bolton Free School flourished until 1874 in the fore-mentioned building that was converted into the rectory.

Pause for a while and explore, in addition to the Priory, the surrounding hamlet of Bolton Abbey, which contains some

The stepping stones, Bolton Abbey

interesting features. The Earls of Burlington and the Dukes of Devonshire were absentee landlords of the estate who contributed to the charm of Bolton, sometimes unintentionally. The archway that spans the Bolton Abbey to Burnsall road, its narrow centre vault a blight to modern vehicles, was built as an aqueduct to the corn mill through the conceit of an Earl of Burlington. Also in the confines of the village stand a splendidly preserved Tithe Barn and the castellated Bolton Hall, which was the Priory gatehouse during monastic times. The outline of the great entrance arch, set within its central tower, is still discernible. It was saved from demolition at the Dissolution, in 1539, by the then Earl of Cumberland, a member of the Clifford dynasty. He converted the gatehouse into a residence and the extensions on either side of the original tower were added in the seventeenth century.

Throughout the year visitors flock to the idyllic setting of Bolton Priory, to examine its remains and to tour the Parish Church. Water level and weather permitting, excited children, often accompanied by protesting parents, tackle the stepping stones that span the Wharfe, as an alternative to the footbridge which provides access to the woodland that coats the steep hillsides on its opposite bank.

One of the finest views of the Priory is obtained from this

Grassington, in quieter times

vantage-point, where it is possible to gaze into the ruins through the east front, which is crowned by a thrusting arch that once contained the mighty east window.

Any one of a selection of paths can be taken through the woods, where a short climb reveals 'bird's-eye' views of the Priory, the river and its scenic environs. The dark mass of Earls Seat appears at closer range, as it looms over the green sward of Strid Wood.

The Way descends from the woods and returns to the riverside as it approaches the Cavendish Pavilion and the nearby entrance to Strid Wood. This recently renovated building and the Cavendish Memorial that stands at the entrance to the Pavilion's access road, provide references to the owners of the estate. Cavendish is the family name of the Dukes of Devonshire.

In an attractive riverside setting, refreshment can be enjoyed within, or outside, the Pavilion café. If a full meal is required, there is also a restaurant. This is a very popular spot, where visitors mingle with walkers, many taking the opportunity to browse in the adjacent estate shop.

Upon entering Strid Wood, a network of leafy paths, laid out in the early nineteenth century, and incorporating a nature trail, can be followed. The paths were the brainchild of the Reverend William Carr, incumbent of the Priory Church for over fifty years. A walk through its verdant alleyways is a delight, particularly in autumn, when colours are at their finest. During that season, the woods are aflame with hues of fiery red, burnished gold and delicate yellow.

The centre piece of the wood is the Strid itself, where the river is pinched, as though by giant fingers, into a narrow channel of frenzied foam, that roars between constricting grit stone rocks. Across this maelstrom, according to legend, the Boy of Egremont tried to jump, fell in and was drowned. It is reputed that his grief-stricken mother, Alice de Romilly, whose family owned the Bolton estate, was moved by this tragic event to grant a piece of land to the canons of Embsay, for the founding of Bolton Priory in 1154.

A mile up the river from the Strid stands the second reminder of Lady Anne Clifford. The tattered ramparts of Barden Tower occupy a mound above the Wharfe, which overlooks the narrow stone hump of Barden Bridge. Originally a hunting lodge, it was one of several within the old Forest of Barden , the favourite hunting ground of its Skipton lords, the Cliffords. The building was enlarged in 1485 by Henry Lord Clifford, known as the Shepherd Lord, because he was raised anonymously on the Cumbrian fells, to escape the Wars of the Roses. He preferred its peacefulness to the splendour of Skipton Castle and spent much time there. He also built the adjacent chapel, which is still intact and currently contains a small café.

Lady Anne Clifford restored the Tower in 1659 and, like her predecessor, spent many of her final years there until her death in 1676, which marked the end of the Clifford line. Since that time the Tower has been allowed to decay, with the exception of some remedial work on its remains in recent years.

The winding riverside path continues, from the shadow of Barden Tower, through rounded limestone hills to the village of Burnsall, which, along with its neighbour, Grassington, is one of the most visited in the Yorkshire Dales. Its car park is usually overflowing and multitudes throng the riverside in the vicinity of sturdy Burnsall Bridge. This mighty overpass seems determined that the fast-flowing river will pass unhindered beneath its substantial arches.

On one auspicious day each summer, all eyes are directed towards Burnsall and Thorpe Fell, which towers above the village. The annual fell race draws competitors from a wide area, as do the associated Sports, which are held in one of the nearby fields. If it proves thirsty work watching athletes strain every sinew and fell-runners scale punishing slopes, only to risk life and limb on hair-raising descents, sanctuary is available in the Red Lion Hotel, once the Bridge End Inn.

Burnsall was an early focal point of Christianity and, sheltered from its bustling centre, stand two notable historic buildings. St.

Wilfrid's Church, its impressive tower prominent against a background of emerald hills, dates largely from the fifteenth century and it contains fragments of Anglo-Danish crosses and an inscribed Norman font.

Its neighbour, a rustic village school, was founded by the 'Dick Wittington' of Wharfedale, Sir William Craven, a native of nearby Appletreewick. Born into poverty, he was determined to rise above his humble beginnings and in his youth he became apprenticed to a mercer in London. He progressed and eventually became Lord Mayor of London in 1611. During his advancement, he never forgot his roots and became a great benefactor to the locality. He rebuilt Burnsall Bridge, funded the restoration of the church and built and endowed the school, which was one of the earliest grammar schools in the country. His memory is perpetuated in the district, for one of the local inns, the Craven Arms in Appletreewick, bears his name.

Just beyond Burnsall the River Wharfe cuts through the craggy defile of Loup Scar, which lies on one of the great Craven Faults. These massive upheavals of the earth's crust produced the wonders of limestone country, such as the incomparable Malham Cove.

Resisting the temptation to linger amidst unspoiled riverside surroundings, our journey continues to a suspension footbridge, which spans the river near some stepping stones. The Hebden Beck, that drains the wasteland of Hebden and Grassington Moors, joins the Wharfe here. A detour beside this now quiet stream would introduce its participants to a wilderness scarred by redundant lead-mining activity. Spoil heaps and disused shafts, litter an area defiled by man, who gave scant thought to restoring the land to its original state. The self-conscious finger of a disused smelt mill chimney stands forlorn on the crest of the moors, a relic of a bygone age, when men clawed a living from the earth and their resultant life expectancy was minimal.

Another vestige of the Wharfedale textile industry manifests itself when Linton Falls are reached. On this site stand the remains of a mill, which, during its long life span produced artificial silk, wool and cotton. The clatter of looms, powered by the energetic Wharfe, has fallen silent, as has the hammering of the mill-workers' clogs on the acoustic surface of the Tin Bridge, as they hurriedly crossed the river to begin their daily stint.

Adjacent Linton village deserves a detour, for it is one of the most refreshing in the Dales. It represents constancy amidst a rapidly-

Packhorse bridge and ford, Linton

changing world. The cluster of houses that surround the tranquil village green, which rolls lazily down to the gentle Linton Beck, appear to have been unaltered for centuries.

A packhorse bridge, which is an absolute gem and ideal photographic material, arches over the beck, alongside its predecessor, the defunct ford, that still remains intact. Fountaine's Hospital occupies pride of place at one end of the green and its impressive features include a cupola and side wings. It was built by Richard Fountaine, as almshouses for the elderly, in 1721.

The Dales Way soon reaches the popular village of Grassington, whose narrow streets and cobbled market-square are a mecca for visitors. It is rooted in early history, for about a mile from its centre lies the site of an Iron Age settlement, occupied from around 200 BC to 400 AD. A medieval village also existed on its outskirts, near Grass Wood and it began to expand when the surrounding estate transferred from the Percy's to the Plumptons in the twelfth century.

The present settlement began to grow with the introduction of lead mining and the textile industry. Now the mines and mills are silenced, it has become a vibrant tourist centre and its popularity has been undiminished since the railways brought eager sightseers from the industrial towns of the West Riding.

Grassington still retains and olde worlde feel, largely due to its picturesque market square, where the village pump, superfluous since the nineteen-thirties, stands stoically beside the convenient seats that provide respite amongst the hustle and bustle. Its importance as a venue within the National Park is illustrated by the Authority's centre situated within the main car park.

As it leaves Grassington, the Dales Way climbs into limestone hills for a scenic, high-level journey to Kettlewell. In the solitude of this upland paradise, the wild grandeur of the Dales unfolds, as the grassy, well-drained footpath is followed.

After an initial steady ascent, the Way levels out and passes the great standing boulder at Lea Green, which marks the site of the prehistoric settlement. Limestone outcrops are numerous and at Coniston Old Pasture, a splendid limestone pavement reveals itself. Vegetation, including small trees, sprouts from the grikes (natural joints in the rock), which create a silvery patchwork. There are protection orders on several such pavements within the Yorkshire Dales, for they are amongst the best in the country. Subject to wind and weather, gradual erosion, encouraged by rainwater, has taken place since the last Ice Age, when the thin layer of soil was stripped from the pavement's surface.

In the limestone folds above the hamlet of Conistone, the path circles the head of a dry valley, known as Conistone Dib. Displaying a wonderful façade of sculptured rock, it cuts deep into the hillside, its stony bed totally dry where once a stream danced on its downward journey to meet the Wharfe.

Immediately beyond this natural wonder of permeable limestone, a wide track is crossed which was traversed during monastic times and possibly earlier. Scot Gate Lane, as the track is known, was used by the monks of Fountains Abbey, whilst travelling through their vast estates, which extended into the Lake District. This particular routeway linked Middlesmoor, at the head of Nidderdale, to Kilnsey, which faces Conistone in the valley-bottom, where the abbey had a grange. The track connects at Kilnsey with Mastiles Lane, which has been in use since the Roman and prehistoric eras. This green lane linked the Cistercian grange at Kilnsey with the Fountains Abbey estates in the northern Lake District. It is currently the subject of controversy, due to its use by four-wheeled drive vehicles that are rendering it deeply rutted.

The next section of the Way reveals exciting panoramas to the north and west. Kilnsey Crag, a prominent limestone buttress, beckons from across the valley. Unfortunately, its distinctive overhanging section is undetectable when viewed from this lofty vantage point. Nevertheless, this knarled, grey cliff cannot be missed as it soars from the lush green valley-bottom like an insurmountable wall.

A little farther up the valley, the River Skirfare meanders through peaceful Littondale to its confluence with the Wharfe amidst patterns of green fields hemmed by striking stone walls. The massive wedge of Firth Fell separates this delightful side valley from the main dale, the dark mass of its moorland crest contrasting vividly with the fertile valleys beneath.

Ahead, Kettlewell can be discerned, nestling beyond limestone outcrops and bands of conifers. Set in an emerald basin, it is flanked by the craggy slopes of Firth Fell and the great dome of Top Mere. Even from this considerable distance, the distinctive packhorse track known as Top Mere Road, can be seen rising behind Kettlewell, as it climbs the lower slopes of Cam Pasture. This wide scar on the landscape scales the open fell pastures to Cam Head.

The current section of the Dales Way and the forthcoming descent to Kettlewell displays limestone scenery at its finest. However, fitness and tenacity are required, in order to tackle the numerous tall, wooden stiles which impede progress. On one occasion I met a walking party, which was proceeding in the opposite direction and whose leader was just mounting one of these prodigious obstacles. Dutifully, I stood aside whilst he and his charges, numbering about eighty, scaled its formidable steps. I was forced to wait patiently for over five minutes before I could continue.

The distinctive sloping roof of the chapel at Scargill House is conspicuous as the steep decline, which returns the Way to the valley-floor, is negotiated. A Church of England conference centre, opened in 1959, Scargill House also provides accommodation and a wide range of holiday activities. It offers a peaceful retreat within unrivalled surroundings.

Kettlewell can be aptly described as the hub of Upper

Yockenthwaite Stone Circle

Wharfedale, for it stands at a junction of roads and has, for centuries, been a natural halt. The old coaching route to Richmond passed through, on its way to Coverdale and Wensleydale. Sheltering beneath the slopes of Great Whernside, whose extensive summit ridge dominates the skyline to the east, Kettlewell was first settled by Ketil in the time of the Norsemen. Rugged fellsides tower above the village, pitted with caves and potholes and scarred by intensive lead-mining activity.

Outstanding views surround Kettlewell, which has received the accolade of appearing on the credits of Yorkshire Television's *Emmerdale*. Those with the time and energy to climb Top Mere Road, will be rewarded with one of the most memorable spectacles of Wharfedale. The prospect over the village and to the south, towards the distant silhouette of Burnsall and Thorpe Fell, reveals one of the shapeliest of grooves in the Dales landscape, that has been symmetrically scoured by glacial action.

Kettlewell was formerly more important than Grassington, but now, like its neighbour, it is reliant on tourism. Drive across the humpbacked bridge in the shadow of the Blue Bell Inn and you will be in the company of scores of motorists wending their way along the dale. Progress is particularly slow in summer, when the streets bristle with sightseers and armies of walkers, who use Kettlewell as a base for exploring the surrounding countryside.

The Dales Way hugs the river as it progresses towards Buckden, overlooked by unbroken ridges that constrain the narrowing valley. A pleasing spot from which to view the river and its environs is the footbridge at Starbotton. Through a delightful avenue of trees, the Wharfe ripples over a shallow bed, its clear waters glistening under a benevolent sun.

A short deviation to the pretty hamlet of Starbotton is worthwhile. Situated on the winding road that links Kettlewell and Buckden, it is bounded by meadows that are a glorious feast of colour in late spring and summer, when wild flowers are at their most prodigious.

It is a mere two miles to Buckden where the windswept moorland of Cray Moss and Middle Tongue splits the dale. Picturesque Langstrothdale branches off northwest towards the heights of Fleet Moss and the market town of Hawes. The main road continues northeast through Cray and Bishopdale to enter Wensleydale near Aysgarth.

Buckden is a focal point for the head of the dale as it is the largest settlement in the area. This upper region, particularly Buckden Pike, is a magnet for walkers and one of the numerous paths to the Pike's summit begins conveniently at the village car park.

Buckden's most prominent building is the Buck Inn, which recalls the former importance of the settlement as a hunting centre. The village's name means 'valley of the bucks' and in Norman times it was established as the headquarters of a great deer-hunting forest. Until fifty years ago it was possible to stroll through surrounding ornamental woods and hillside bracken and be rewarded with the sight of grazing fallow deer. These animals freely roamed the estate until it came under new ownership.

Disregarding Cray and the climb up the Kidstones Pass, the Dales Way veers into Langstrothdale to traverse the upper reaches of the Wharfe. Its journey through this scenic valley is marked by serene landscapes and undisturbed beauty.

At the gateway to Langstrothdale stands the hamlet of Hubberholme, where, from its dignified bridge, an inspiring view of Buckden Pike is obtained. On either end of the bridge sit Hubberholme's two most significant properties; St. Michael's Church and the George Inn, formerly the vicarage. The squat, but graceful tower of the church still retains Norman traces and inside is a rare oak rood loft, that dates from the mid sixteenth century. Such lofts were eradicated during the Reformation, but this one survived because of Hubberholme's secluded position. The familiar wooden mice, trademark of Robert ('Mousey') Thompson of Kilburn, can be found carved into pew ends and J.B.Priestley is buried in an unmarked grave in the churchyard.

There are two choices of route to tiny Yockenthwaite, one of the many settlements named by the Norsemen, who inhabited Langstrothdale. The pastoral riverside can be followed, or the more energetic can climb the abrupt hillside to examine the former Quaker meeting place at Scar House. This interesting building provides ample compensation for the short ascent and it has occupied its lofty position since 1698.

From Scar House, a rough, stony track, requiring stout footwear and sure-footedness, provides a fitting high-level alternative to the river route, for it provides superb views along Langstrothdale's wooded flanks. Across the valley, the high watershed of Birks Fell and Horsehead Moor, that separates the head of Littondale from Langstrothdale, can be clearly seen. These two valleys have been linked by ancient trackways since the Bronze Age.

The track from Scar House eventually descends to the dainty stone bridge that spans the narrow Wharfe at Yockenthwaite and shortly after the valley-bottom route is rejoined, a compact stone circle is passed. This ring of thirty small stones lies in a riverside meadow, now a playground for lambs. It was constructed during the Bronze Age and is reputed to stand on what was an ancient trade route over the Pennine watershed.

Between Yockenthwaite and Deepdale, the river keeps close company with the narrow road and this part of upper Wharfedale is much favoured by motorists, whose cars often line the roadside verges. They can be seen strolling along the riverbanks, or enjoying riverside picnics.

At Deepdale, a tightly knit collection of farms, the road crosses the river by means of the narrow Deepdale Bridge and just beyond stands a footbridge which overlooks a familiar Dales scene. The sturdy farm at New House squats by the river, its weathered stone front inset with rows of pocket-sized windows. In its shadow, the vibrant river has cut into its multi-layered limestone bed to form a miniature Strid. The farm and its attendant bubbling channel appear on many postcards and calendars.

The source of the Wharfe is less than two miles from this spot and from hereon, the enthusiastic infant river cascades over numerous delicate waterfalls. A steady gradient leads to the meeting of the Greenfield and Oughtershaw becks, where the river begins its long haul to the North Sea. This location provides a fitting climax to the journey through Wharfedale. The neat farmhouses of Beckermonds shelter amongst a gallery of hardy trees that sway softly in the bleak wind amidst a stunning background of High Pennine fells.

CHAPTER SEVEN

Who Said That History is Dull?

Who has not at sometime been jolted from slumber in the small hours of the morning, filled with dread at the thought of an impending speech at a forthcoming function or meeting? I am certain that it has happened to most of us. One of the exceptions is Ian Dewhirst, although it may be that in his early years he suffered like the rest. Public speaking holds no terrors for Ian, who can talk on a variety of subjects, for as long as time will allow, with barely a pause for breath. Such an accomplishment has to be earned of course and in Ian's case it represents the fruits of years of study and research into what was once his work and is now his passionate hobby.

He was born in Keighley in 1936 and has lived all his life in the gritty industrial town that lies in the heart of the Aire valley. His home surroundings and its people have provided a continual source of inspiration over many years and Ian enjoys the coveted accolade of being admired by another accomplished Yorkshireman. Bill Mitchell, author and editor of the *Dalesman* for almost forty years until his retirement in 1988, relates with relish that every time he arrives at a venue to present a lecture he is asked if he knows Ian Dewhirst. He is made to feel inferior by his host, who proceeds to tell him, 'Ian gave a talk here last week and he <u>was</u> good.'

Anyone who portrays such a passion for his subject is bound to succeed and Ian has the knack of gripping an audience without reliance on script or illustrations. History courses through his veins and in his retirement it forms as great a part of his life-blood as the nearby River Aire.

Ian asserts that his appetite for delving into the past was nurtured during his formative years, for it was his grandparents who provided the spark that ignited historical ambitions within him. His paternal grandmother and maternal grandfather died when he was very young, but his surviving grandparents, Grandfather Dewhirst and Grandmother Slater, promoted Ian's keen sense of history by providing a rich fund of reminiscences.

Both surviving grandparents were accomplished musicians and

Grandpa Dewhirst played the double-base in Keighley War Hospital during the First World War, providing encouragement to musically inclined wounded soldiers. He once told of playing in an entertainment for wounded soldiers from the Boer War, which made Ian prick up his ears, as did another of his grandfather's tales which concerned a local murder that had taken place at Guard House, near Keighley in 1864. Ian was taken by his grandfather to the spot where the murderer had hidden, in the Lower Holme Mills goit alongside the North Beck. This encouraged the impressionable boy to unearth more about the gruesome occurrence, that became known as the 'Greenhouse Farm' murder.

Grandpa also took Ian to places where he had spent his own boyhood, including the little mill at Dunkirk, near Oxenhope, relating that in those days little boys wore petticoats and he had sat on top of a stove in the mill and set his petticoats on fire.

Grandmother Slater had been a cinema violinist during the silent-film era. In addition to background music, she sometimes provided sound effects. One of her stories concerned the silent film *The Lost World,* based on the story by Sir Arthur Conan Doyle, which included prehistoric animals. Whilst this was in progress, she had to contribute the sounds made by pterodactyls!

For many years Grandma was a violinist in the Keighley and District Orchestral Society and she proudly recounted the occasion in 1903 when she was conducted by the great Samuel Coleridge-Taylor. The renowned composer had agreed to conduct the Keighley Musical Union, when they performed his 'Hiawatha,' at the request of J.B.Summerscales, one of its leading members. This was somewhat of a 'scoop,' as the composer did not normally make a practice of conducting amateurs. Grandma Slater played in the First Violins as a member of the Orchestral Society, thus providing her with a lasting memory and Ian with another family story that opened his eyes wider to history.

The Mansion House Museum stood near to Grandma Slater's home, occupying part of the former mansion that was once the home of a prosperous mill-owner. Here Ian discovered a treasure-house of natural history, Egyptology and military regalia. From then onwards he went to the museum as often as anyone would take him and ever since has been unable to resist such places.

Another place that Ian remembers with affection is Grandma Slater's kitchen, a popular family meeting place, which sported a huge table and a cavernous, glass-fronted bookcase containing a diverse array of works, collected by Grandpa Slater. These ranged from meaty volumes by Lamb, Scott, Carlyle and Macaulay to Victorian Sermons and old guides to the Lake District. This bookcase exerted an incalculable influence on his development and indirectly it was Grandpa Slater, whom Ian had barely known, who awakened a cultural and literary awareness within him. Somehow Ian sensed his grandfather's very presence in those books.

One of his abiding memories of Grandpa Slater is his contention that the writing desk, subsequently passed to Ian, once belonged to Robert Southey. However, there are apparently several similar desks, currently located in Keswick museum, that are also purported to have belonged to Southey, who became Poet Laureate in 1813. Ian adds another twist to this story through his perusal of family letters and memorabilia, which involves the Banks family, of Keswick. His mother's antecedents included a branch of this family, who owned a pencil mill in the Lakeland town. A surviving Banks family letter of 1843 recounts 'Poor Mr. Southey died this morning' and goes on to give Southey family details. Unfortunately Ian has not yet been able to verify any family connection.

Ian has outlined reminiscences of his childhood and beyond in a collection of essays entitled *You don't remember Bananas*. A strong thread of humour permeates this book and many of his reflections provide a chuckle, not least because one can identify with the situations he describes.

In this highly readable volume he recounts wartime experiences that strike a chord with all those who lived through such austere times. He tells of his father, serving in the R.A.F, tending barrage balloons in such far-flung corners of the Empire as Accrington and Scapa Flow. A 'senseless up and down business,' was how his father described the task of looking after the 'gas-bags,' as they were commonly referred to.

From a memorable visit to Blackpool in 1940, that took place whilst his father was undergoing basic training, three incidents remain firmly implanted in Ian's mind. His father 'square-bashing' on the promenade. A fellow-airman passing by with blood dripping copiously from his hand, which he had inadvertently impaled on his own bayonet, and a dark revolving drum among the South Shore amusements, that anyone brave or, foolish enough, could attempt to crawl through. Ian's father took him through this rotating orifice

Grandfather Dewhirst in the orchestral band – he is on extreme right

amidst a welter of bodies tossed around like corks and flying missiles torn from defenceless pockets.

Warlike gangs of young scalliwags existed around the country during those dark days, which fought imaginary battles with the most bizarre weapons. Keighley had its quota and Ian joined his local band, complete with toy 'tin-hat' and a Navy belt into which he stuck his most prized possession, a brightly-painted wooden sword. He entered a world of make-believe Errol Flynns and Gene Autrys, an exciting addition to air-raid drills, gas masks, Saturday matinees at the local pictures, German POW's, Red Cross parcels, lurching tanks and blackout curtains. Life was never dull for that band of ragamuffins.

A peculiarity of life is that an incident, seemingly trivial at the time, can add a new dimension to our existence. So it was on the day that Ian used the convenience belonging to Old Pheasey. This rather distinguished gentleman was a friend of Grandfather Dewhirst, having been a regular customer in Grandpa's newsagent's shop, which incidentally still bears the name 'A. Dewhirst and Sons.' Grandpa always refered to him as 'Old Pheasey,' so his real name remained a mystery. During a family visit to Starbotton , a charming hamlet in Wharfedale, to which the old weaving overlooker had

Ian at Hebden Bridge

Meadows near Wensley, Wensleydale

Grassington market square

Cliffe Castle Gardens, Keighley

The Mansion House Museum

moved on his retirement, Ian paid his one and only visit to Old Pheasey's convenience. This whitewashed edifice stood at the top of the wickedly sloping back garden and behind its neatly painted door hung the remains of a cheap edition of *Chico the Jester* by Alexander Dumas.

Toilet paper was a valuable commodity in those days and many of the book's pages had been torn out and used for more urgent purposes. Ian began a cursory glance through its remains and became so engrossed that he sat enthralled until anxious calls wafted through the garden demanding to know his whereabouts. Thus his taste in reading was profoundly influenced at an early age and he was prompted to search for cultural sustenance.

From a neighbour he acquired a set of Arthur Mee's eight volumes of *Big Books for Little People,* a set of children's Encyclopaedias that purported to 'make your life happy and good.' At school he made frequent use of the book cupboard, from which could be chosen, at any one time, a volume contained within its storehouse of literature. Out of this Aladdin's Cave came a wealth of enjoyable reading, such as *Tom Sawyer, Black Beauty* and *The Last of the Mohicans.*

An additional bonus, in the form of the Yorkshire Dales, entered

Ian's life at this juncture. His father had been demobbed from the R.A.F. and those immediate post-war years were to provide freedom and exploration on a grand scale, for he had launched into motor-cars and travel began in earnest. Free from the restrictions of modern traffic-jams and congested country roads, every outing contained the thrill of adventure, even to the extent of bouncing along rutted tracks, not knowing if you were driving up a blind alley.

Ian revelled in these exciting ventures that revealed the sweeping landscapes of the Dales. He began to wonder what lay across the fields and up the hills and where the tumbling streams began their lives. To find out he took up walking, which, he discovered to his delight, was the ideal way to experience the sights and sounds of the countryside.

To be accurate, these were not the first of Ian's trips to the Dales, for he recalls being taken by tandem, at a very early age, on a tiny seat wedged between his mother and father. Unfortunately he was too young to appreciate his surroundings and remembers very little of these episodes, apart from receiving a nasty dose of 'cobble-rash,' inflicted by his parents. This occurred when he was pitched onto a market square (Grassington, he thinks) as his mother and father pulled up and dismounted. Unluckily for Ian, neither one of them held the tandem firmly upright as he waited to be lifted off. Both parents strenuously deny the story, but Ian asserts that he can still see those cobbles rushing up to meet him.

When his time at Keighley Grammar School neared its end, Ian secured a place at university to read English. The time had come to leave the nest and its familiar surroundings and step into an unknown academic world with its prospect of enforced self-reliance. However, he was not required to travel a great distance. It was fortunate that he had no time for the Wars of the Roses because he went o'er the tops to the University of Manchester. This became his domicile for three years and he only returned to Keighley for his vacations.

Graduation eventually approached and the spectre of National Service, which had been deferred until his studies were completed, began to loom large. Another transition was quickly upon him. 'I do not know what lies before me. I go out into the world tomorrow,' mused Ian on his last night as a civilian. On the following traumatic day he shrugged off his youthful chrysalis and entered manhood as 23575232 Recruit Dewhirst of the Royal Leicestershire Regiment.

During that summer of 1958 the sun shone gloriously for weeks on end whilst Ian trained as an infantryman, complete with camouflaged helmet. No toy 'tin-hat' this time, things were for real. The Almighty must take a delight in pouring sunshine onto raw recruits as they struggle and sweat, in full kit, through punishing training routines. I speak from experience because the previous summer I had done my basic R.A.F. training in exactly the same conditions.

'Square-bashing' completed, Ian was transferred to the Royal Army Educational Corps, in deepest Buckinghamshire, to undergo training as a sergeant-instructor. Here the officers lived a superior life-style in a faded mansion that is said to have once belonged to Disraeli, whilst Ian and his comrades existed more primitively in Nissen huts scattered within the estate. These huts, Ian was told, appeared unwittingly in a prominent television series that was being filmed at a nearby film studio. His abiding memory of his time there was the 'full glory of autumn,' as he expressed it, 'that lent colour and beauty to our regimented squalor.'

Qualification as a fully-fledged instructor brought another posting to Blackdown , near Aldershot, where he was attached to the Royal Army Ordnance Corps. He busied himself with classes, inspections and the unit library, attaining the impressive position of Garrison Librarian.

One Sunday afternoon Ian wandered into the surrounding woods and although it was the trailing-edge of winter, the heat was tangible and the earth felt warm. Assuming that it would still be cold and hard in his native Yorkshire he was moved to spontaneously compose a poem embodying the contrast between the Northern and Southern climates. It is one of many that Ian has compiled over the years, but it has the rare distinction of being completed at one sitting.

A short time later Ian was moved from his grubby battalion education rooms into the more palatial No. 8 Army Education Centre, to specialise in teaching English. Life distinctly improved as he exchanged the strict routine of the Sergeant's Mess for an idyllic hut amongst a garland of trees, surrounded by squirrels, hens and the odd cat or two. He describes its occupants as an assortment of individualists. These included an elderly Grenadier sergeant who carried a tame magpie around perched on a stick and a sinewy R.Q.M.S. whose hobby was constructing miniature gardens from broken bricks and leaf-mould.

Dunkirk Mill, Oxenhope

Although he was enjoying his more relaxed lifestyle, Ian was frequently homesick and recalls gravitating to books about Yorkshire during frequent trips to the bookshop that stood at the top of Guildford High Street. This regular haunt was crammed with books of every description that even flowed out onto the pavement. Despite his longings for home and family he formed some strong friendships and surprisingly found himself reduced to tears when demob arrived and he had to say goodbye to his comrades.

Ian returned to Yorkshire, never again to live outside the county.

Though he may not have realised it at the time, his spell in the army developed the lecturing skills that were to serve him so well over the succeeding years.

On his return to civilian life Ian began his association with Keighley Public Library, where he worked for thirty-one happy years. After seven of those years he was appointed Reference Librarian, which provided unlimited access to a wealth of archive material and allowed his personal interests to dovetail with his work. He became one of those lucky people whose job also became his hobby. His exhaustive research permitted him to forge personal links with the history of his locality and particularly the people within it. Ian asserts that although book history played a significant role in his endeavours, he learnt much from family letters and newspaper cuttings, one of which, he recalls, was a memorable piece describing

A tandem made for three. Ian is the youngster in the middle.

the Great Exhibition of 1851.

Many of the interesting local characters that he unearthed exerted a profound influence on him, not least amongst them being Gordon Bottomley, whom Ian describes as 'Keighley's forgotten poet.' His great-niece donated much of his material to Keighley Library and this was influential in promoting Ian's crusade of reconstructing forgotten lives. Bottomley left Keighley at the age of eighteen and came to prominence as a member of the Georgian Poetry movement, a literary group that was active just prior to and during the First World War. His work, however, spanned more than one period, from the late Pre-Raphaelite lyricism of the 1890's, through the Georgian Poetry period to experimental verse-drama between the wars. Two of his literary friends were John Masefield, with whom he experimented with a garden-theatre and Edward Thomas, who was killed at Arras in 1917. The letters sent by Thomas to Bottomley are preserved in the form of a published collection. Although he was highly regarded in literary and artistic circles, Bottomley was not universally acknowledged, for the literary quality of his life and work have tended to put him out of reach of the general public.

Sometimes, when Ian refers to Gordon Bottomley during a talk, the audience laughs as though it is a joke. He can only assume that Bottomley may sound a funny name to strangers, or that they confuse him with his contemporary, Horatio Bottomley, who died in infamy and poverty after serving seven years' penal servitude for fraud.

Another of Ian's favourite characters, who could have been torn from a Dickens novel, was John Milligan (1812/ 1876), a respected local doctor and medical officer to the Keighley Poor Law Union. A great campaigner for health care and social improvement, he also served as medical officer to the Keighley Board of Health, established in 1855. Keen to get his message across, he was an enthusiastic lecturer, a key topic being, 'Poverty as a source of Disease.' He was also a poet and a writer and one of his works, penned in 1861, was entitled *Baal : or Sketches of Social Evils; a Poem in Ten Flights.* This ran to 210 pages, with sections on Drink, Physics, Mammon, Cant, Matrimony, The Church, Justice, Politics and Elocution, with Moral Reflections for good measure! Not content with a heavy workload, he even found the time to indulge his life-long interest in Geology.

During his time at Keighley Library Ian pursued his numerous outside interests, including the Brontë Society, of which he has been a member for forty years. It is the district and its people, at the time of the Brontës, that holds the greatest fascination for him and he has researched many of Haworth's characters, highlighting their lives in articles and talks given to Society members. Unsung heroes are once again very much to the fore, such as Joseph Hardaker (1790/1840), poet and druggist in Haworth, who had first-hand knowledge of the Brontë family, counting Patrick and his son Branwell, amongst his friends.

Ian's love of walking has taken him to all parts of the Dales, where he has revelled in its ever-changing vistas and quiet solitude. Although he enjoys being a member of Keighley Holiday Fellowship and an occasional walk leader, Ian admits a preference for lone walking, which offers the freedom to progress at his own pace and wander at will. He also confesses to developing an elitist attitude towards his coveted Dales. Exposure to television coverage, he feels, has over-popularised certain areas and he prefers to keep away from the throngs that now invade the 'honey-pots.' He has branched out into other districts and is currently enjoying the countryside of South Yorkshire, which has revealed a hitherto unimagined beauty.

Early retirement in 1991 allowed Ian to concentrate on his writing and since that time he has produced several books, numerous articles and newspaper columns. Such diverse subjects have flowed from his typewriter as the histories of a local paper-tube manufacturer and the Keighley and District Orchestral Society. The former, J. Stell and Sons Ltd. required a piece for their brochure that

The start of a Walking Match near Keighley

celebrates the company's 125 years in business. For the 100th anniversary of the latter, Ian was invited to dive into the Society's annals and produce a resumé of its century of life.

In addition to articles for a variety of magazines, Ian contributes a weekly piece for the *Keighley News* entitled 'Down Memory Lane.' If his articles are of the same quality as his writings in *You don't remember Bananas* they are certain to amuse and entertain. On purely selfish grounds I highlight a further passage from this delightful publication because it holds a particular poignancy for me. It is entitled 'Confessions of a Peripatetic Public Speaker' and it is written with the aid of thirty-eight years' hard-won experience as a lecturer. It is a hoot. I laughed at each subtle observation of the pitfalls that await the unsuspecting lecturer at many of his venues. Most of those that he describes have happened to me. Having travelled to countless desolate-looking premises on dark, wintry nights, I can confirm that salt can be well and truly rubbed into your wounds as you arrive to find the place in pitch darkness. Feeling wretched after a tortuous and interminable journey, during which you have managed to lose your way several times, you wonder if you have got the wrong night. Two minutes before the scheduled start of your talk a figure appears out of the gloom, full of apologies and swearing to being accosted by Jehovah's Witnesses. It is the ever-faithful Speaker-Secretary who is at pains to explain the lack of participants. You are assured that *This is Your Life* is just finishing and hordes of people will arrive at any moment (this usually applies to 7-30 p.m. starts; for 8p.m. one substitutes *Coronation Street*). All this to contend with and the talk has not even begun!

The demand for his talks is as great as ever and Ian inevitably has to disappoint some of his many applicants. By way of illustration of his depth of knowledge, not to mention sense of humour, let me list some of the intriguing titles.

Kruger's Coffins and the Great Humming Beetle.

Yorkshire Life Between the Wars.

The First World War on the Home Front.

The Second World War on the Home Front.

Life in Victorian Yorkshire.

Yorkshire Dialect Poetry and Prose.

Keighley 200 Years Ago

Haworth at the Time of the Brontës.

History Through Postcard Messages.

The last title may seem a rather obscure subject, but Ian, who has a fascination for them, reckons that 'entire epochs are captured in a mass of trivia and occasional drama on their backs.' Whilst you and I would merely admire the pictures on their fronts, he picks out cryptic messages, such as the following, penned by unknown senders.

'When you send parcel, please send six packets of baking powder.'

'Send undershirt as soon as it is ready.'

'Please dear bring plenty of towels as we are coming in bathing with you next week.'

Ian's talents have not gone unheeded, for in 1996 he was awarded an honorary Doctorate of Letters by The University of Bradford. This was granted in recognition of his services to local history and to the town of Keighley. At his investiture Ian was greatly surprised by the oration that was presented on his behalf. He describes it as a *This is Your Life,* for the orator had carried out exhaustive research into his subject, just as Ian has done for many others.

CHAPTER EIGHT

The Farm Beside Baildon Moor

It is an exhaustingly hot day and the sandals on your feet chafe mercilessly. The hirsute habit, that is your everyday attire, feels like an oven and you long to remove the irritating itch between your shoulder blades, that is maddeningly out of reach. Dust from the rough track along which you are trudging billows around your legs and you long for the peaceful confines of your abbey that lies many miles away. This is the harsh life of an abbey retainer entrusted with touring the extensive monastic estates to ensure that things are in good order and the tenants are keeping up with the rent.

As you pause for breath a welcome sight meets your eye. It is Faweather Grange, one of the many such outposts scattered throughout the lands of your domicile, Rievaulx Abbey, that nestles at the foot of the North York Moors. You heave a sigh of relief, throw off your pack and mop your brow, relishing the thought of sustenance and a night's rest.

Several centuries pass and on that identical spot by the side of the track, which now forms part of the York to Manchester packhorse route, a solidly built farmhouse stands. It is the late seventeenth century, the monks are long departed and the farm is beginning its life sandwiched between the bracken-coated slopes of Baildon Moor and the busy section of trade route that the track now comprises. Two stone cottages, which have replaced the monastic grange, can be seen at nearby Faweather.

At the time of writing this story, the farm has evolved into a building of character, which, despite modification, still retains many of its original features. The track by which it stands, known as Sconce Lane, is little changed since monastic times, apart from some patches of weathered stones worn smooth during centuries of chafing by countless feet and hooves.

The isolation from metalled roads, which the farm affords, has proved to be a blessing and also a hindrance to its present longstanding occupants. These are two brothers, both bachelors. Its secluded and elevated position provides a kaleidoscope of views,

Baildon Moor

which include extensive tracts of windswept Baildon Moor. On a clear day one can see far beyond the urban sprawl of Leeds to the stark outlines of the great cooling towers that serve the power stations many miles to the east. These are set in a vast green landscape that stretches towards distant York and Goole. Nearer to hand, the course of the Gill Beck can be detected as it eases through a lush wooded valley to merge with the River Aire near the village of Esholt.

The brothers moved to the farm with their parents in 1937 from nearby Baildon, when their father lost the tenancy of his farm in the village, due to the acquisition of his land for building purposes. This was a bonus to the growing boys who enjoyed the more isolated setting of their new home, free from traffic and disturbance. Despite the arduous conditions, they enjoyed their newfound freedom. Calor gas, which provided power for cooking and lighting, had only recently become available and the fact that electricity did not make its appearance at the farm until 1953 was of no great concern to two lively boys, who had plenty of activities to occupy their time.

Not frightened of hard work, they became energetically involved in the exacting tasks that farm life presents. With the exception of a brief period spent in hospital by one of them, the brothers have never spent a night away from the farm. Having no desire to live anywhere else, they have remarkably never taken a holiday, considering them unnecessary.

One drawback to their isolated existence has been the difficulty of access to school, shops and amenities. There was no provision of transport to school in the nineteen-thirties and school dinners were unheard of. The boys walked into Baildon for lessons and had to carry their lunches. If funds permitted, they could squander a halfpenny at Mrs. Nicholson's sweet shop; a rare treat.

Sconce Lane is a rough thoroughfare, requiring careful negotiation by vehicles and their current means of transport is a small van that is used only for indispensable journeys. During the extremely harsh winter of 1947 the lane was impassable for nine weeks, with deep snow even burying the surrounding stone walls. Life had to carry on and a living still had to be made, so the resourceful family resorted to a horse-drawn sledge for transporting milk for sale in Baildon. At that time snow clearance in outlying areas had to be done by hand and the brothers can remember twenty men arriving one day with shovels and digging a track across Baildon Moor through daunting snowdrifts that threatened to envelope them.

The sale of milk and eggs played a significant role in the farm's economy during those austere times, and if deliveries were missed, severe hardship loomed. For many years door to door deliveries were made in the village both morning and evening. These necessitated long working days that commenced with milking in the early morning and ended with deliveries around the village in the late evening.

During the Second World War a substantial amount of crops were grown, as all farms were required to do, in order to provide food for a hungry nation. Even allotment holders and households were encouraged to grow as much food as possible through the popular 'Dig for Victory' campaign. The farm's fields were given over to cereal crops and turnips and kale were also grown to provide much needed cattle feed. In addition to dairy cattle, a variety of livestock was kept, including pigs and poultry, which helped their self-sufficiency.

The lack of amenities on the farm, such as power, has already been outlined, but this is only part of the story. Water is still obtained from a well on its land, for no mains have ever been laid. Various mechanisms have been used to draw water from this source, which

Baildon in the 1960's

was first tapped in 1903. Prior to that time a borehole had to be used. Initially, a wind pump extracted water from the well and supplied it to storage tanks in the barn. One of these tanks still remains in its loft. A hydraulic ram pump was eventually tried and persevered with until 1940. Unfortunately it proved unreliable and was replaced by a more satisfactory petrol engine that also provided power for the milking machines when they arrived. Water is now obtained by courtesy of a modern electric pump.

During the years when hand labour was still widely used, their father employed three farm hands, but had to release one of them when milking machines were introduced. A further concession to mechanisation came in 1951, when a tractor replaced the horses and ended forever the skill of wielding scythes. This innovation did, however, eliminate many hours of back- breaking toil, particularly at harvest-time.

Sixty years of life at the farm has provided the brothers with a store of memories, both of the locality and their immediate neighbours. The miners' cottages at nearby Sconce had been pulled down shortly before their arrival, when coal-mining, that had taken place on Baildon Moor, was terminated. They have witnessed the

The army entertaining themselves on Baildon Moor.

transformation of the site into a modern camping and recreation centre used by scouts and guides from a wide area. No longer sleeping under course blankets and cooking over open fires, the youngsters of today enjoy the benefit of the modern amenity buildings that supplement the tented accommodation.

A local character, Ted Richardson, who was renowned for his dry humour, was most indignant when electricity was supplied to the campsite. In his opinion, it was no longer camping when such conveniences were provided. A man turned up at Ted's house one snowy night and enquired if he could pitch a tent in his field. He was promptly told, 'If you have a house, go to it, or if you have a car, sleep in it!'

Another neighbour, Maggy Addingham, spent all her working life at Salts Mill in Saltaire, then a major source of employment in the area. Every working day, without fail, she walked the seven miles there and back, always arriving promptly for work. The exercise obviously did her no harm, for she lived to the grand age of ninety. Maggy would be amazed to witness the restoration and subsequent re-birth of her former workplace, which now attracts visitors from around the world.

The brothers remember the days when visitors to Baildon Moor made a beeline for Aunt Aggie's, a neighbouring wooden building that served as a café. There they enjoyed refreshment provided by Aggie and her husband, whose speciality was mouth-watering oatcakes that were hung over the fire to mature. Sadly the oatcakes are long gone, for the building was demolished in1970, its modern counterpart being a lone ice cream van sited in the moor's main car park.

Near the farm lie the remnants of an extinct quarry that formally yielded high quality flag and building stone, used for many buildings in the locality, including Ilkley Town Hall and Bradford City Hall. During the quarry's working life the brothers became accustomed to the clatter of quarrymen's boots as they passed the farm twice daily on their routine march. The quarry has been landscaped and its site is currently occupied by holiday chalets, which provide a quiet haven.

A standing stone in one of the fields adjacent to the farmhouse recalls former times when the boundaries of surrounding lands were jealously guarded, to the extent of landowners riding the perimeters of their property annually in order to ensure their authenticity. During the eighteenth century, one over-zealous landlord erected boundary posts around his land and rode his borders with a shotgun at the ready. Evidence of demarcation exists in the form of an inscription 'W.T's B's,' on the afore-mentioned stone, which is believed to be one of thirteen such boundary stones erected by William Thompson, who was Lord of the Manor of Baildon from 1784 to 1839. The inscription is most likely an abbreviation of 'William Thompson's Boundaries.'

Many of the brother's memories encompass the Second World War, but they recall an incident that happened a few years earlier, when, in 1935, they watched in awe as the renowned airship, 'Hindenberg' soared above Baildon Moor. They were convinced that it was on a reconnaissance mission in preparation for war, which, prophetically, proved to be only four years away.

During the uneasy peace that immediately preceded the outbreak of war, they recall the emergence of gas masks and the daunting ordeal of donning these claustrophobic appliances at school, supervised by their teachers. How pitiful they must have appeared, those lines of elephantine youngsters, snorting through their man-made trunks and squirming in discomfort as their tutors walked amongst them, checking that the masks were sufficiently tight fitting.

The demise of the popular Baildon Carnival in 1939, due to the imminence of war, was a severe blow. It formed a traditional highlight of the pre-war years, providing an annual week of revelry, processions and concerts. When the Carnival lights were extinguished for the last time, the brothers felt that it signified the end of an era.

In the turbulent years of conflict that followed, the adjacent moor and golf course were commandeered by the army and soldiers of the 5th Duke of Wellington Regiment were billeted in austere huts on it. Their duties included aircraft spotting and they had a powerful searchlight for use at night, in addition to one small anti-aircraft gun. The soldiers' arrival caused a stir amongst the local populace and crowds arrived to witness the army in action, of which, unfortunately, there was very little.

A rather bizarre set of wooden poles were erected at that time, apparently to prevent enemy gliders landing on the moor. In the early days of the war, the British constantly feared invasion, but thankfully, the gliders never materialised. What was probably the most dramatic incident of the war, as far as Baildon and its moor were concerned, occurred when a German bomber screamed over the district one dark night in 1941, spurting fuel and flame as it dived towards oblivion. It finished its downward plunge in a suburb of Bradford, five miles away.

After Hitler's defeat things returned to normal and the soldiers disappeared from the area. To placate deprived golfers, who had either been away fighting, or had suffered severe withdrawal symptoms, a further three holes were added to the golf course, which was restored to its former glory.

If German bombers had ever blackened the skies over Baildon Moor, the farmhouse possessed a ready made air raid shelter in the form of the cavernous cellar that lies deep beneath it. Hewn from solid bedrock, it is accessed by a flight of stone steps, concave from three centuries of wear. The surrounding rock and the thick walls above ensure that it remains strikingly cool, thereby providing an adequate alternative to the modern refrigerator.

Another distinctive feature of the building is its windows, many of which are attractively mullioned. Two small ones light the cellar steps and have shouldered-arched lintels that are a delight to the eye. Unfortunately one of these windows is partially obscured, as its lower half is below ground level, the result of modifications carried out to the farmhouse in the mid-eighteenth century.

Other problems have been experienced with the building over the years. Shortly after its erection it was discovered that large items of

Farmhouse window with shouldered-arched lintel

furniture could not be manoeuvred up the stairs and that the bedroom windows were too small to pass them through. To overcome this oversight, the builders made a hole in the sitting room ceiling and fitted a trapdoor to allow furniture to be hauled through. Later improvements rendered the trapdoor obsolete and it is now thankfully sealed.

Having experienced the changing pattern of farming over many years, the brothers, although not decrying the progress that has taken place, feel that not all the changes have been for the better. They sense that the influx of restrictive legislation and regulations has complicated what has always been to them an enjoyable and rewarding occupation.

The farmhouse

Sconce Lane

View towards Esholt from Baildon Moor

Baildon Moor in winter

'William Thompson's Boundaries' stone

They derive great pleasure from their weekly trip to Otley market, which has for many years provided their main source of entertainment. It is their link with the world at large and the place where they can meet with their counterparts and keep their finger on the pulse of farming in the area.

The brothers also enjoy the occasional chat with passers-by, like myself, who often meets them as I walk along the lane on my way to Ilkley Moor. They are very knowledgeable, despite their cloistered existence. As an indicator of changing social patterns, they observe that fewer people walk past their farm than in former times. All is not lost to the motor car, however, for they have also noticed that the number of passing cyclists and runners is on the increase.

Very few people can look back with satisfaction upon sixty years of living in the same house, forsaking holidays and relying on the occasional trip to market. Immune from our rapidly changing times, life progresses much the same as it has for decades at this farmhouse with its unique occupants, stimulating setting and rich store of memories. Who would decry the modest, yet fulfilling, lifestyle of these two extraordinary gentlemen who provide a lesson to all those who adopt a materialistic attitude.

CHAPTER NINE

The Underrated Dale

I hold a sneaking affection for unsung Nidderdale, one of the least publicised of the main Yorkshire Dales. Whilst visitors flock to Wharfedale, Wensleydale and the bustling villages of Haworth and Malham, this scenic valley quietly beckons the discerning traveller.

A place of great beauty and variety, it lies just outside the boundary of the Yorkshire Dales National Park, hence the quiet solitude of its upper reaches. Many people believe it to be a dead-end valley, which is partially true, because the motorist cannot venture further than Scar House Reservoir, which is secreted at its head. This expansive water-source and its neighbour, Angram Reservoir, are ringed by untamed moorland, topped by the imposing domes of Great Whernside and its smaller version, Little Whernside. However, a little further down the valley, at Lofthouse, there is an exit road that takes a scenic path to Wensleydale. It passes the serene Leighton Reservoir before threading through a cluster of tiny villages to arrive at Masham. At Pateley Bridge, situated roughly at the mid-point of the dale, several roads emanate to neighbouring dales.

There is something to attract everyone along the course of the River Nidd that rises on the flanks of Great Whernside and glides amongst lush meadows to join the River Ouse near York. Described as the 'Switzerland of England' in the nineteenth century, it offers everything from weathered sandstone crags, sweeping panoramas and unspoilt villages, to tracts of wild heather-clad moorland.

The adjacent towns of Knaresborough and Harrogate, that form a gateway to the dale, need no introduction for they are well known in their own right. They have been popular since visitors flocked to the variety of healing wells to 'take the cure.' The local chalybeate and sulphur springs were considered by the Victorians to be highly efficacious and valuable remedies for restoring strength after illness or improving the blood.

Knaresborough is a town steeped in history, which still retains a medieval and Tudor flavour, through its historic castle and ancient market-place, surrounded by narrow streets, which are overlooked by

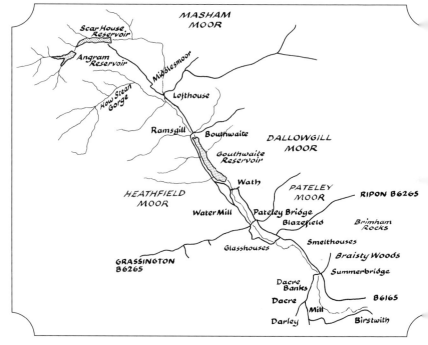

Nidderdale – Summerbridge to Scar House

buildings of significant age and character. The remains of the castle, perched high on a rocky buttress, overlook the broad sweep of the River Nidd and the famous nineteenth-century railway viaduct that spans it. Mother Shipton, the renowned prophetess, adds another dimension to the town. She was born in a cave beside the magical Petrifying Well over 500 years ago, but her legend lives on. The Cave and Well draw countless visitors and they lie within the Mother Shipton Estate that incorporates beautiful riverside walks.

Nearby Harrogate deserves the title of the 'Floral Capital of Nidderdale,' for in summertime it is resplendent with colour as you walk the broad pavements or admire the blooms of the Montpelier and Valley Gardens. Set in what was formerly the medieval Forest of Knaresborough, the hunting grounds of Norman barons and English monarchs, the town began to develop at the end of the eighteenth century around the springs that were being discovered. The coming of the railways in the mid-nineteenth century had a dramatic effect on its growth and by the end of the century its population had trebled. Harrogate became a fashionable resort and many of the fine

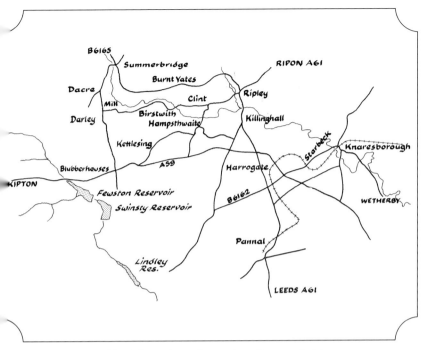

Nidderdale – Knaresborough to Summerbridge

buildings on view today sprang up at that time. Attractive stone terraces, imposing hotels and grand public edifices gave the town an aura of refinement and respectability. These have provided an ideal legacy that has engendered the popularity that the resort currently enjoys.

If you venture through Nidderdale's inviting gateway and take the B 6165 road from Knaresborough an enticing journey of twenty-five miles to its head beckons. Initially the road passes the Nidd Gorge, a deep, wooded valley, containing delightful riverside paths and nature trails. Rhododendrons add splashes of colour to the verdant confines of Bilton Woods, within which there is a bird sanctuary. The sedate brown waters of the river are strewn in places with the tangled foliage of fallen trees, but more importantly for fishermen they contain a rich supply of brown trout and grayling. Occasionally, the meandering river becomes more animated and bubbles over pebbly beds, intent on enjoying its passage through the leafy channel.

As you pass through the hamlet of Nidd, from which the dale takes its name, the province of the Ingilby family is entered, whose home has, for six centuries, been nearby Ripley Castle. This historic building stands on a grassy knoll, overlooking a glistening ornamental lake in the midst of rolling parkland, landscaped by Capability Brown. It presides over the model village of Ripley that was built to resemble those of Alsace-Lorraine. The original thatched cottages were replaced in the early nineteenth century by Sir William Amcotts Ingilby, who built the neat stone houses which survive today. These give a unique character to the village, as does the rugged market cross, sited in its cobbled centre. Ripley has the rare distinction of having a village hall bearing the name of Hotel de Ville. The local post office currently occupies part of this distinctive building, which adds to the appeal of this seemingly timeless settlement.

The Boar's Head Hotel, that overlooks the market cross, owes its origins to the Ingilby family. In the fourteenth century, King Edward was hunting in the Forest of Knaresborough when he was alarmingly thrown from his horse into the path of a wild boar. He was only saved by the prompt action of Thomas de Ingilby and showed his gratitude by conferring a knighthood upon his host, who adopted a boar's head as the family crest.

This is a convenient point for walkers to join the Nidderdale Way, which passes along the main street of the village. This long-distance path circles the dale, weaving an intricate pattern as it alternately hugs the riverside, searches out the scenic nooks and crannies of the valley-sides and traverses the high fringes. The fifty miles, or thereabouts, of its paths, tracks and occasional stretches of road form an ideal route on which to explore this peaceful dale. One word of caution; delightful though this footpath is, the standard of way marking in certain sections could be improved. It is essential to take a good map, or guidebook of the area and to keep a careful lookout for direction signs.

The next stage of the journey up the dale, from Ripley to Summerbridge, constitutes an inspiring high-level drive, for after passing through Burnt Yates, a green and pleasant landscape unfurls. Nestling below is a pattern of neat stone farmsteads, their fields enclosed with dry stone walls and a scattering of stone barns within them. This is a view unique to the Yorkshire Dales and unfortunately, the influx of large, modern farm sheds is eroding the traditional lodgings for cattle, who are housed on the ground floor of the barns, whilst their winter fodder is stored on the floor above.

Beyond this idyllic setting, an extensive panorama stretches towards the head of the dale, where meadows give way to heather-clad moorland and brooding fells. In summer, the sheep, which have been a mainstay in the economy of the dale since monastic times, crop the higher pastures and fells. The monks of Fountains and Byland abbeys grazed extensive flocks on the same land, home to the indigenous red grouse, curlew and lapwing.

This inspiring view not only demonstrates why Nidderdale has been designated an Area of Outstanding Natural Beauty, but it compels the visitor to traverse the whole length of the dale without pause until the lofty amphitheatre, that encloses Scar House and Angram reservoirs, is reached.

If exploration of a more leisurely nature is preferred, you can walk beside the river for much of its length, or enjoy strolling through the abundant woodland that flecks the valley-floor. If you traverse the open fields in winter your reward may be the sight of flocks of redwings and fieldfares, heads bobbing as they pick their way across the pastures in search of food.

The pastoral expanse of the lower dale is dotted with old settlements, where life has altered little over the centuries. Many nestle by the river as it courses through the valley below Pateley Bridge, a demarcation point within the dale. The Nidd has provided power for the numerous mills that formerly lined its banks. These were used for a variety of purposes, including the manufacture of flax and rope and the grinding of corn. Many still remain, unused or converted for other purposes. For example, the former cotton mill still remains at Birstwith, but it is now used by a food processing company.

Several riverside settlements date back to the time of the Doomesday Book and the hamlet of Clint, near Ripley, was established during the time of the Vikings. This tiny hamlet still retains its distinctive stocks and the base of its ancient market cross that huddle together at the roadside, seemingly isolated. These historic landmarks are an indicator that Clint has declined in size and status.

Hampsthwaite, a neighbour of Clint, has even older origins. It stands on the line of the Roman road that linked Ilkley with Aldborough, near Boroughbridge. On the outskirts of the village stands a shapely stone bridge that marks an important crossing point of the Nidd. During Roman times it was necessary to ford the river and the first bridge probably appeared in medieval times, when the village had an important market. In the era of packhorses and

Ripley Castle

stagecoaches, the bridge lay on the route from York to Manchester and it is a fine example of seventeenth-century craftsmanship. At the time of its construction, the bridge was linked by a causeway to the rolling acres of Ripley Park. A section of this ancient thoroughfare has recently been unearthed, but its age has proved hard to determine. Its origins could date back to Roman times, but today it provides an impressive approach to the Ripley Estate, permitting splendid views of the imposing castle and the neighbouring church.

A short distance up river from Hampsthwaite lies Birstwith, its pleasant buildings scattered within an appealing tree-studded setting. The view of the village from the riverside is particularly rewarding. Here the Nidderdale Way ambles through lush meadows, heavy with dew on atmospheric spring mornings. In conditions such as these the walker can discern the gracefully tapered church spire emerging from the low-lying haze like a slender pyramid.

A walk along this stretch of the Nidderdale Way is delightful

'New Bridge' at Birstwith

The Panorama Walk, approaching Pateley Bridge

Pateley Bridge

Rainbow near Middlesmoor

Brimham Rocks

when the autumn foliage coats the riverbanks with a profusion of colour. Set amongst this arboreal splendour is an elegant, high-arched bridge of 1822 vintage. Built in the familiar packhorse style, it replaced an earlier version that appeared at the end of the sixteenth century. Steeply humped to allow the passage of floodwater, it must have presented a daunting obstacle in its early days. Initially, this type of bridge was without parapets, or had only low ones, to facilitate unobstructed passage for side-slung panniers on the packhorses that clumped across it.

The villages of Darley, Dacre and Dacre Banks stand a little way from the river as it curls towards Summerbridge. On the outskirts of Darley stands Darley Mill Centre, a former corn mill that houses an exhibition, craft shops and restaurant. Its restored waterwheel and millrace add a further attraction to this fine example of the dale's industrial heritage.

An intriguing variety of building styles adds to the appeal of this trio of villages and several stone-built properties date back to the seventeenth and eighteenth centuries. Dacre occupies the former site of a grange for Fountains Abbey and its neighbour, Dacre Banks, that lies closer to the river, evolved in the nineteenth century with the expansion of its several mills.

Just across the river from Dacre Banks lies Summerbridge where the B 6165 road, that runs up the dale from Ripley, is rejoined. This thoroughfare forms the main street of the village and on the hillside above stand rows of millworkers' houses, built in the nineteenth century when the textile trade was at its height. The prime force behind the evolution of Summerbridge was the prosperity of the successful New York Mill, which was built in 1825 on the outskirts of the village. Today none of the inhabitants work in the mills, which have fallen silent.

Adjacent to the crossroads in the centre of the village stands an inn bearing the unique name of the Flying Dutchman. It is sited on what was the medieval road from Fountains Abbey to its grange at Dacre and at that time the whole district was owned by the influential abbey.

Many of the farms that surround Summerbridge are of seventeenth-century origin and they were built shortly after the granting of 1000 years leases to their occupants by the Ingilbys of Ripley, who were in need of capital at that time.

A narrow, winding road climbs from the crossroads up the steep valley-side towards Brimham, passing Braisty Woods on the outskirts of the village. Here a delightful network of paths thread through quiet glades, thickly carpeted with bluebells in springtime. On warm days a leafy canopy of oak, yew and larch offers welcome shade, whilst lilting birdsong rides on the air. Willow warblers, siskins and redpolls, the migrants that return each spring, join the chorus of perennial inhabitants, such as finches and thrushes.

Braisty Woods was the home for generations of the Skaife family, who were originally keepers of the local grange for Fountains Abbey. Oak bark, for tanning, was obtained from these woods by the Skaifes, who rebuilt the grange and enlarged it in the early eighteenth century and who carried out their trade on the site.

One of the wonders of Nidderdale beckons beyond these woods, drawing the eye towards their lofty setting on the valley rim. I refer to Brimham Rocks, the widely renowned boulders of millstone grit, weathered over thousands of years into a series of weird and

Yorke's Folly

remarkable profiles. Now under the guardianship of the National Trust, they teeter on the edge of Brimham Moor, seemingly about to plunge from their perch and cut a swathe through the valley-side. There is a convenient car park on site, from which a series of paths snake amongst the unique outcrops.

From the superb vantage point of these rocks you can survey a tapestry of emerald fields and silvan clusters that stretches into the upper dale. The distant moorland that encloses the deep cleft of the valley head reveals itself and closer to hand, across the valley, the metal finger of a mast that balances on Abraham Crags, can seemingly be touched by the outstretched hand

Above the village of Glasshouses, that snuggles in the valley bottom, between Summerbridge and Pateley Bridge, runs one of the most scenic sections of the Nidderdale Way. It passes rows of delightful stone cottages that cling to the hillside in the hamlet of Blazefield, which is aptly named. Here you pass gardens that are ablaze with colour when rhododendrons, laburnum and lilac are at their most prolific.

Looking down on the amalgam of houses and cottages that

comprise Glasshouses, you are conscious of its industrial origins. It expanded in the nineteenth century when the Metcalfes began their flax-milling business and like Summerbridge, its legacy is lines of mill houses built by a local entrepreneur.

By the side of the B 6265 road, which leaves the valley road (B6165) beyond Glasshouses and winds up the hillside to Blazefield, stands a sign indicating Knott and the Panorama Walk. From here, a track, and eventually, minor roads, lead to Pateley Bridge, along the line of the Nidderdale Way. It is a splendid high-level journey, of approximately two miles, that requires stout footwear and good visibility. The rewards are magnificent, particularly in springtime, when you pass between mature stone walls and hedgerows, replete with hawthorn blossom, that border fields bedecked with the yellow hues of gorse and buttercups. Cow parsley and sinewy grasses wave in the breeze on lush verges and the air tastes clean and fresh as you enjoy an elevated parade. As you begin to descend, you are rewarded with 'birds-eye' views of Pateley Bridge. Across the valley, the rocky promontory of Guise Cliff can be seen, protruding above copses, thick with larch, birch and rowan. Beyond this distant mecca for photographers stand the gaunt, crumbling pillars of Yorke's Folly, twin towers of local stone, built nearly two centuries ago to provide work for the local unemployed. Constructed at the instigation of the local Yorke family to resemble a Rhineland ruin, one of its original three towers was destroyed during a violent storm in 1893. A convenient seat is provided near to the remaining towers, which is a boon to visitors who have accomplished the demanding climb from Pateley Bridge. Here they can rest whilst admiring the panoramic view and recovering their breath.

If you are feeling fit on your arrival in Pateley Bridge, you can extend your walk and return to Glasshouses by means of an opportune riverside path.

The town of Pateley Bridge can be described as the hub of upper Nidderdale. It is familiar to many motorists, for it lies on one of the popular routes through the Yorkshire Dales. Several roads converge here, permitting convenient access to numerous towns and villages in the area, including Grassington, Skipton and Ripon.

Its narrow streets hug the hillside beneath the barren remains of Scotgate Ash Quarries, which, together with the local lead mines have been largely responsible for the town's growth and prosperity. Despite the demise of these industries, Pateley Bridge is a bustling place for many months of the year, thanks to its location on the Yorkshire Dales tourist trail.

The Nidderdale Museum was established in the town in 1975, to ensure that the traditional life of the dale is not forgotten. Amongst the many displays are recreations of local life, embracing industry, crafts and customs of a bygone age. Also featured are illustrations of the harnessing of the dale's greatest resource, its ample water supply. They show the construction of the great reservoirs that occupy much of the upper dale.

The reliance of the valley's development on the railway is also demonstrated in the museum. It was the expansion of the lead mines in the early nineteenth century and the arrival of the railway that put Pateley Bridge on the map. The irrepressible Metcalfes, who were involved in most ventures in the locality, were instrumental in the building of the North East Railway that provided a link with the line already serving Leeds, Harrogate, Ripon and Thirsk. As early as 1818 Thomas Telford surveyed a line to Pateley Bridge, but it was George Metcalfe III who got the project underway. Following his acceptance as a shareholder in the venture he was told that providing he could raise half the capital and negotiate the necessary land, the railway would be built. He achieved this target in six months and eighteen months later the line to Pateley Bridge was opened.

It is possible to trace sections of this now dismantled railway, which followed the winding course of the River Nidd. Parts of its overgrown embankments are clearly visible from the riverside paths. In addition to providing an outlet for the millstone grit of Scotgate Ash Quarries, owned by the Metcalfes, the line also promoted the distribution of dairy produce to nearby towns and cities. It inevitably increased tourism, attracting visitors to the dale from a wide area.

An incline was constructed at Pateley Bridge, which ran from the stone quarries down to the valley bottom and connected with the railway, to aid the handling of blocks of millstone grit. Sadly, after all the hard work and ingenuity that went into the enterprise, the North East Railway closed in 1963.

Pateley Bridge today is not merely a place to drive through on a Dales tour, for it offers the visitor numerous attractions. Not least of these, is its steep and narrow main street, bordered by appealing buildings that house busy shops and cafés. Viewed from the town's most familiar landmark, its shapely bridge over the Nidd, this frequently photographed thoroughfare exhibits an air of timelessness.

How Stean Gorge

Attractive riverside parkland adds to the charm of Pateley Bridge. Bewerley Park, is the venue for the annual Nidderdale Show, but unfortunately it is not open to the public on a regular basis. However, the municipal park on the opposite side of the bridge is always available.

Many paths radiate from the town, rendering it a good walking centre. There are riverside walks, or, for the more energetic, climbs to the stone quarries, or Yorke's Folly and Guise Cliff. It is also a convenient point to join the Nidderdale Way, which passes through the town centre.

Pateley Bridge heralds a distinct change in the character of Nidderdale. From this point the valley begins to constrict until it becomes a deep channel that is ended abruptly by the man-made stone rampart of Scar House Dam. As demonstrated in the Nidderdale Museum, the upper valley has been converted into a gigantic water store, where towering dams distend the youthful Nidd and capture the issue from countless moorland streams. The chain of three reservoirs, Gouthwaite, Scar House and Angram was a far-sighted innovation, instigated at the end of the nineteenth century to provide water for distant Bradford and its environs.

Road and river keep in close contact until the village of Lofthouse is reached. Here, the valley splits, at the junction of the How Stean Beck and the Nidd.

Between Pateley Bridge and Gouthwaite, the first and oldest of the reservoirs, lie interesting echoes of earlier times. The Nidderdale Way bisects the old lead mine workings on Greenhow Hill as it leaves Pateley Bridge and curves away from the river and traces a broad loop. It passes through a a derelict landscape of spoil heaps and disused shafts before turning towards the Nidd once more as it heads for the hamlet of Low Wood. When the mines were in full swing in the 1830's, two-thirds of the male population of the nearby village of Bewerley, and one quarter of that in Pateley Bridge, were employed there.

Another example of the area's industrial heritage can be seen as you drive along the narrow, winding road that travels up the dale from Pateley Bridge. The Watermill Inn comes into view just before the tiny humped-back bridge, that spans the Foster Beck, is crossed at Corn Close. This impressive hostelry was formerly the Foster Beck Flax Mill, named after the watercourse that provides power for its massive waterwheel. The recently restored thirty-four feet diameter wheel occupies pride of place at one end of the converted mill. It was

A contractor's special train between Lofthouse and Scar House

used for driving machinery until 1967 and now merely rotates for the benefit of onlookers.

It is a short journey from Corn Close to Gouthwaite Reservoir, which is preserved as a private nature reserve. Here, the eye is drawn to the twin stone pillars that flank the entrance to impressive Gouthwaite Lodge. This gateway reveals a two miles long expanse of water lying in an unadulterated pastoral setting. Its tree-lined fringes, overlooked by verdant hillsides, are reminiscent of a Lakeland valley. Completed in 1899, the reservoir was responsible for the demise of Old Yorke Hall, the former seat of the influential Yorke family. Prior to the flooding of this section of the valley, the building was dismantled and the stone used to build a Tudor-style house that can be seen by the roadside as you drive past the reservoir. It was discovered, on completion of the house, that there was enough stone left to build another property, so a farm was built on the hillside behind the house. This is shown on the Ordnance Survey maps as Gouthwaite Farm.

The reservoir is popular with bird-watchers, as it lies within a bird sanctuary. There is little opportunity to see the birds from the narrow road that runs beside the reservoir, unless the viewing facility is used that is provided near to a car park and picnic area. However, a public bridleway runs along the opposite side of the reservoir, from Wath to Bouthwaite, from which a better view of the birds can be obtained.

The stoneyard and works at Scar House

Larks, sandpipers and pipits can be found breeding by the shore and for company they have the water inhabitants, such as mallard, tern and swans.

At the head of Gouthwaite Reservoir nestles the historic village of Ramsgill. In monastic times a grange for Byland Abbey was situated here, for the abbey owned much of the surrounding land and also the extensive flocks of sheep that grazed it. The Abbot established a chapel, of which, only the gable end remains. It stands unobtrusively behind the present church, which occupies a commanding position overlooking the reservoir.

The settlement's connection with the Yorke family is recalled by the ivy-clad Yorke Arms which occupies pride of place beside the village green. Attractive white stones encircle the sections of the green, which are enlivened by a picturesque stone cross and a shapely drinking trough.

One of the most notorious characters in the history of Yorkshire, Eugene Aram, was born here, of humble parentage, in 1704. He became an accomplished scholar and founded a school in the village. After a time he moved to Knaresborough and began a school there. His reputation was shattered, however, when he was implicated in a scandal involving fraud and a dubious colleague who had apparently absconded with a large sum of money. Some years later Aram was suspected of murdering his vanished partner in crime and his troubles were compounded when a skeleton was found in a local cave. He was arrested and tried at York Assizes, where he was convicted of the brutal crime and sentenced to death. The sentence was carried out at Knaresborough, where he was hung on a gibbet. This gory episode aroused enormous public interest and not only was it featured in a novel by Bulwer Lytton, it inspired a poem by Thomas Hood, which ran thus:

> Blood for blood atones!
> Aye, though he's buried in a cave
> And trodden down with stones
> And years have rotted off his flesh
> The world shall see his bones.

This poem encouraged a trail of Victorian tourists to visit the area and Henry Irving contributed to Aram's notoriety by portraying him on the stage.

A short drive up the valley from Ramsgill brings you to Lofthouse, a former Norse settlement and the site of another grange belonging to Fountains Abbey. Adjacent moorland is still referred to as Fountains Earth. The monks of Byland Abbey were also active in the area, excavating for lead and grazing sheep.

An attractive war memorial fountain stands in the centre of the village. An inscription upon it advocates the 'use of cold water – inside and out.'

The only road to escape from the upper dale climbs from the village up Trapping Hill and sets a course for Wensleydale. Two minor roads come to a halt at the neighbouring hamlets of Middlesmoor and Stean. Yorkshire Water permits the use of the narrow waterworks road, on payment of a small toll, which continues to Scar House at the head of the dale. Before taking that road, Middlesmoor and the How Stean Gorge are well worth a visit.

The former perches on a shoulder of land that separates the River Nidd from the How Stean Beck and its elevated position affords one of the finest views of the upper dale. Stand in the grounds of the graceful fifteenth-century church and on a clear day you will be rewarded with a vista that stretches far beyond Gouthwaite Reservoir. Ambitious walkers may wish to climb the steep, grassy path that leads from Lofthouse, to end virtually at the door of the church. Guaranteed to make you perspire, it has the bonus of revealing ever-widening views of Nidderdale. If you need to recover after your exertions, there is a tearoom handily situated near the

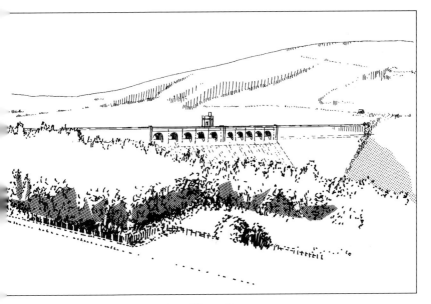

Scar House Dam

church, or, you can leisurely examine the church itself, which was licenced in 1484 and contains a medieval stone cross.

If the climb to Middlesmoor is too strenuous for your tastes, it can easily be reached by car, or, you can drive the short distance from Lofthouse to the impressive How Stean Gorge. Here you can wander along narrow paths through a seventy feet deep fissure of sculptured limestone and admire galleries carved in the rock faces by centuries of erosion. Convenient bridges span the ravine; excellent vantage points from which to observe the How Stean Beck scouring its bed an alarming distance beneath you. There is a restaurant and tearoom on site, should you feel in need of fortification after your adventure.

The waterworks road, which leads to Scar House Reservoir, also offers its own brand of fulfillment, for a drive along it is extremely rewarding, particularly in autumn. In that season, the avenues of trees that intermittently line the road form corridors of scarlet, yellow and gold. The approach to the mighty castellated wall of Scar House Dam is punctuated by the russet hue of bracken that coats the steep valley sides as they curve up to sepia tinted moorland.

An equally gratifying means of access to this spectacle is provided by the shooters' track that traverses the valley rim by way of Dale Edge. This wind-blown gash through all-pervading heather accords sweeping views of the upper dale and also of Scar House Reservoir. Access to this track is obtained by following the Masham road out of Lofthouse for roughly one and a half miles.

Yet another admirable alternative exists. The Nidderdale Way, after leaving Lofthouse, offers a walk of rich variety as it heads for Scar House. Its path alternately hugs the River Nidd, glides through embracing woodland, or traverses the abrupt valley side. On the low-lying section, the gnarled, stony riverbed can be clearly seen in places, the water having permeated through the indigenous limestone. At other times the sun filters through leafy canopies to dance on limpid pools, filled by tumbling streams. It is an area of potholes and caves and the river disappears at one stage into Manchester Hole, a vast cave, 600 feet in length. When there is a sufficient flow of water, the excess from Manchester Hole is carried several hundred yards to Goyden Pot, where it is swallowed once more. From these two caves the river travels underground, to re-emerge near Lofthouse.

As it approaches the halfway point between Lofthouse and Scar House, the Nidderdale Way begins a scenic climb as it follows a great curve of the valley to within sight of the majestic Scar House Dam. It passes a series of farms perched high on the hillside, whose inhabitants enjoy spectacular aerial views of the valley.

If fatigue is taking hold and Scar House seems an eternity away, welcome refreshment may be found at Thwaite House that lies directly on the path. This inviting farmhouse overlooks Goyden Pot and a small roadside car park, handily situated for visiting Manchester Hole. Refreshment is served in the attractive garden, but only at weekends, in fine weather. You will need the time and the elements on your side if you are looking for respite here.

The walks over Dale Edge and along the Nidderdale Way to Scar House involve distances of six to seven miles and in addition, a return journey to Lofthouse awaits. If it can be arranged, the most convenient method is by car, using the Waterworks road. For those intending to walk back, the Nidderdale Way can be followed to Middlesmoor, by way of a moorland track and from there a descent can be made of the previously mentioned steep path to Lofthouse. A walk along the Waterworks road is a less adventurous alternative, but it can include the bonus of verges bedecked with colourful canopies of willow herb, saxifrage and campion.

At elevated Scar House you enter a silent world. Apart from a handful of buildings there is only windswept water, enveloped by the lonely habitat of grouse and curlew. Untamed beauty surrounds you on the roof of Nidderdale, but how different was the scene earlier this century. Noise and industry were the order of the day around a settlement consisting primarily of workmen's dwellings. This was the time when the dams for the two great reservoirs of Angram and Scar House were under construction. For thirty years this activity continued, Angram being completed in 1914 and Scar House in 1936. Amidst scenes of sweat and toil ran the Nidderdale Light Railway, built to connect with the North East Railway at Pateley Bridge, in 1904. It carried much of the stone used to build the dams, which was supplemented by the excavation of a small quarry, the remains of which is visible on the rim of Woodale Scar that overlooks Scar House Dam.

As you step from your car in the car park that is provided near Scar House Dam, evidence of former habitation and activity surrounds you. A village of 1250 inhabitants was built here during construction of the dams. Ten large hostels housed the workmen and bungalows were provided for foremen and technicians. Many amenities were available, such as a school, concert hall, cinema, church and a small hospital. Set into the base of Woodale Scar are the remnants of bunkers and, on the plateau beneath, the foundations of buildings, arranged in tiers, are clearly visible.

The overgrown remains of the railway sidings lie a short distance away that mark the line of the Nidderdale Light Railway, which ran to the base of Angram Dam. It was originally a private line for Bradford Corporation and even operated a passenger service until 1929. Its demise came in 1936 when Scar House Reservoir was completed. What a pity it is not in operation today for I feel it would make a popular tourist attraction.

Those who wish to explore further can initially walk along the parapet of Scar House Dam and take in the unrivalled view from its ramparts. The great curve of the valley obscures much of upper Nidderdale but what remains is adequate compensation. The river squirts from the base of the dam 150 feet below and wriggles through the thick garland of variegated vegetation that comprises Scar Plantation. Conifers mingle with ash, beech and hazel and slivers of woodland fragment from this tunnel to career up numerous fissures in the hillsides that harness tinkling streams. Above this verdant scene the eye can range over the rugged expanse of Masham Moor.

A network of tracks and paths provides further opportunity to explore the deep basin that encompasses Scar House and Angram reservoirs. Sections of this network encircle Scar House Reservoir and a path can also be taken which leads onto the slopes of Great Whernside and eventually crosses the watershed to descend into Wharfedale.

This remote setting signifies the end of a journey through Nidderdale. It is a rewarding one that contains a wealth of interest and scenery of the highest calibre.

CHAPTER TEN

That Surprising and Wonderful Man

Are you beginning to feel your age? Do you consider that the allotted three score years and ten is a good innings? If either of these is the case, take heart and visit the village of Bolton on Swale. There, in the churchyard of St Mary's Parish Church, you will find a monument to the memory of Henry Jenkins, reputedly Yorkshire's oldest man, who made the normal life-expectancy of seventy years seem a very short span.

He was born in the neighbouring tiny village of Ellerton on Swale in 1500. History relates that he spent all his life in the locality and finally expired at the ripe old age of 169 years. Ellerton and Bolton lie at the edge of the pastoral Vale of Conyers and Mowbray, that is sandwiched between the Yorkshire Dales and the North York Moors. Walkers may be familiar with Bolton on Swale, for it lies on Wainwright's popular Coast to Coast Walk. It is situated six miles from Richmond and one mile from Catterick Bridge, where the long-distance footpath crosses the A1 motorway.

Henry was born into an age of discovery, when horizons were broadening and hitherto unknown continents were being unearthed. Columbus was in the midst of his global voyages, having recently discovered Trinidad and the mainland of South America. Other great seafaring explorers were also very active. Vasco da Gama became the first European to open up the sea route to India during an expedition from his native Portugal. A little earlier, he had sighted Natal on the South African coast and also discovered Mozambique. The Venetian, Cabot, sailed on a voyage of exploration to Newfoundland and Nova Scotia, believing them to be part of Asia. His countryman, Sebastian Cabot, subsequently journeyed in search of the North West Passage and entered Hudson Bay.

It was also a time of progress in science and the arts, particularly music. The violin family of instruments made their appearance during the year of his birth, together with the earliest form of harpsichord known as the virginals. The Dutch were developing pumping machinery to help drain and reclaim some of their land

and the coiled spring for operating clocks was invented in Nuremburg. British activity included the establishment of the Press in Fleet Street, which was to become one of our great national institutions.

The modern age is considered to be the most rapidly changing one, but Henry must have observed many remarkable developments during his extensive life-span. One of his earliest remembered activities was taking a horse, loaded with arrows, to Northallerton for supply to the English army, which marched to Flodden Field in 1513. Henry recalled the incident with pride many years later, for the Scots were defeated at the battle, mainly through the efforts of the formidable English bowmen.

He lived to see a total of nine monarchs on the English throne. His birth occurred during the reign of Henry VII and he survived until that of Charles II. In the interim period Henry VIII, EdwardVI, Jane, Mary, Elizabeth I, James I and Charles I all came and went. Despite Henry VIII's philandering and monetary meddling, he was, in Henry's opinion, the most memorable. This is a remarkable tribute considering that this is the king who caused rampant inflation by his dispersal of his predecessor's fortune and his debasement of the coinage.

During the reigns of this imposing list of monarchs, Henry would have recollections of many great events, such as Drake's world voyages and his battle with the Spanish Armada. Another memory would be of the Pilgrim Fathers setting sail from Plymouth in 1620 for the New World. He lived through the Civil War, which began in 1642, when fellow-countrymen fought each other and the monarchy was temporarily destroyed. Towards the end of his life there occurred, in relatively quick succession, the Great Plague and the Great Fire of London in the mid-1660's. At that time, Sir Isaac Newton was conducting his experiments on gravitation and evolving his revolutionary mathematical theories.

Also at that time, land was in great demand. It provided the major source of employment to a population that was gradually rising following the ravages of the Black Death, when a third, or possibly one half, of the inhabitants of the kingdom died of the plague in less than two years.

Henry's earliest memory relates to accompanying his father to market with his horse and cart to sell vegetables. At the age of eleven or twelve he left home to escape his father's temper and beatings.

St Mary's Parish Church, Bolton on Swale

*The monument to Henry Jenkins in the graveyard of
St Mary's Parish Church*

The inscription on the monument to Henry Jenkins

The Henry Jenkins Inn, Kirkby Malzeard

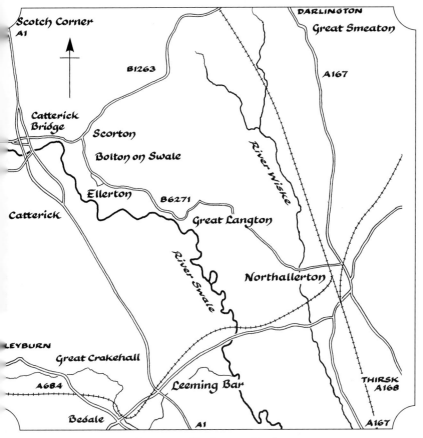

Location of Bolton on Swale

After jobbing for two years he was taken into the service of a local gentleman called Mills. He rose to become footman and eventually butler and stayed for a period of roughly twelve years. Henry then obtained the situation of butler to Lord John Conyers of Hornby, Constable of Richmond, who had led the local contingent at the Battle of Flodden. During that period he had frequent contact with the monks of Fountains Abbey through the carrying of messages for his master. He became friendly with them and they gave him roast beef and strong ale. Unfortunately, these times lasted for only a few years as the monasteries were soon to be dissolved and the last Abbot, whom Henry came to know well, had to sign the Deed of Surrender.

After the death of Lord Conyers in 1557, Henry earned a living by fishing in the River Swale and he continued to do this for over

100 years until 1661. He often swam in the rivers and it is recorded that he crossed the Swale in spate when well past his century and swam in it for many more years.

Henry was finally persuaded to retire at the age of 161 by the local gentry who considered him too old to work and somewhat of a celebrity. They kindly supported him during his remaining years by the provision of food and a small dole.

When he was 163 he was persuaded to dictate his life history to Mrs. Ann Saville who had moved to Bolton on Swale and heard of Henry's great age. Sceptical of the tales that she had been told, she decided to obtain the true facts from the man himself. Henry was not averse to revealing his memoirs to the lady, who subsequently wrote an account of them. These were published as a short volume and many years later a copy was found by accident amongst some old books purchased at an auction in York. It was already very old, for it was printed in Old English and had become badly faded and worm-eaten. The purchaser could, however, make out that it bore the signature of Mrs. Saville and he set about transcribing it into a legible form. From his enquiries he found that it had long been out of print and he decided to re-publish it under the title, *The Life and Memoirs of That Surprising and Wonderful Man, Henry Jenkins.* A claim appears on the title page stating that it is the only genuine and authentic account of the man commonly called 'Old Jenkins,' a nickname that had been widely used during his latter years by the people of the district. Another statement describes Henry as 'The Oldest Man to be met with in the Annals of England.'

A copy of this revealing book is held in the Local Studies section of Bradford Central Library. It tells how, initially, his grandmother and then his mother became self-styled village 'doctresses.' This came about through his great uncle, who had been a ship's surgeon, giving his drugs, medical apparatus and treatment book to his sister when he had no further use for them. Expert medical attention was, at that time, the province of only the rich, and people from the surrounding area consequently flocked to his grandmother when anything ailed them and likewise to his mother after her death. Henry gave the treatment book entitled *A Collection of 604 Valuable Receipts* to Mrs. Saville as he had no use for it, being unable to read or write. The collection of remedies is quite an eye-opener and it gives a good indication of how treatments have changed over the years.

He did, however, have a good knowledge of cures for various

ailments and swore by certain precautions and remedies, to which he attributed his longevity. The wearing of flannel next to the skin was one such precaution, to be followed both in summer and winter. If this was done when young it would ward off old age and prevent the limbs from taking cold. The custom had been passed down through generations of his family and may have been the reason why none of them ever suffered from gout or rheumatism and all lived to a great age. His sister, for example, who was two years older than Henry, died when he was 113 years old.

His diet consisted of plain food, such as bread and cheese, or cold meat with onions. Raw onions, he maintained, were very beneficial in many respects, including promoting sleep and warming the system. Henry only ate when hungry and drank when thirsty, seldom drinking anything but water or small beer. Occasionally, after a hard day's work, he would drink a pint of strong beer, but, in his opinion, the regular consumption of strong and spirituous liquors constituted a slow poisoning of the system and led to premature death. The best water to drink, he advised, was rainwater, caught in an earthen pan. After settling it could be drawn off clean into another vessel and kept sweet for a long time. 'Early to bed and early to rise,' was another of his maxims, which he adhered to all his life and a half-hour walk after supper was always taken to assist the digestion before retiring to bed.

Whether or not these habits were truly beneficial can only be judged by their results. Because all the family enjoyed good health and retained full use of their faculties throughout their long lives, they were not without merit. Mrs. Saville recorded that Henry, although a great age at the time of his dictation to her, displayed clear thought and a good memory.

No-one can be absolutely certain that Henry survived to such a great age, but, according to Mrs. Saville, an intelligent authoress, who was converted from her scepticism, Henry could clearly remember facts from his early life, which add weight to his claim. Other facts, quoted by Henry during his interview, helped to convince Mrs. Saville that he was telling the truth. Henry always gave his age as approximate, whereas an impostor would have been more definite. He maintained that his mother told him that he was born in 1500, but, due to the absence of parish records at that time, he could not definitely authenticate this fact.

Henry's recollection of the Battle of Flodden and the fact that he knew King Henry was away fighting in France at the time and that

THE
ONLY GENUINE AND AUTHENTIC EDITION
OF THE
Life and Memoirs
OF THAT
SURPRISING AND WONDERFUL MAN
𝕳enry 𝕵enkins
COMMONLY CALLED
OLD JENKINS,
Of Ellerton - upon - Swale in Yorkshire

WHO LIVED TO THE ASTONISHING AGE
OF
169 YEARS AND UPWARDS
WHICH IS
SEVENTEEN YEARS LONGER THAN OLD PARR
AND THE
Oldest Man to be met with in the Annals of England

Written from his own dictation at the Age of One Hundred and
Sixty-three Years,

BY MRS ANN SAVILLE
Of Bolton, in Yorkshire,

Where a Monument is erected to his Memory by Public Subscription.
an Abstract of which was published in the 3d vol.of the
Philosophical Transactions, and is likewise
under his Print, by Worlodge.

PRINTED FOR THE EDITOR
BY J.A. GILMOUR, MARKET PLACE, SALISBURY.

Title Page of book by Ann Saville

the leader of the British troops was the Earl of Surrey indicate that he was born before 1513. He could not have read about such events because, as stated previously, he had never learnt to read.

Another fact that aids Henry's claim is that when Lord Conyers, whom he served for some years, died in 1557, Henry's name was listed amongst his servants, which confirms that he must have lived for at least 120 years.

Henry's local knowledge, especially concerning land ownership before the anarchy and confiscations of the Civil War, was used at court hearings, which he was often summoned to attend. There were records in the King's Remembrancer's Office, in the Exchequer, of his appearance as a court witness, such as in 1655 at Kettering, in Yorkshire. He was also frequently at York Assizes, to which he travelled a distance of fifty miles, on foot. Here, in 1655, he testified, on oath, that he remembered a right of way to be in existence in 1540 and Henry's age and evidence were never questioned during cases concerning tithes at Catterick in 1667.

Henry swore in Chancery and other courts to possessing above 140 years memory, in fact it is recorded that he once proved that a father was 140 years old and that his son was 100. Several other elderly witnesses at court hearings testified that they knew Henry Jenkins and that he was already very old when they first knew him.

If you get the chance, do visit his monument in Bolton on Swale churchyard. This imposing edifice, erected through public subscription in 1743, towers proudly above the surrounding gravestones. His still-discernable name is carved on its base. Inside the charming fourteenth-century church you will find a large tablet of black marble on the south wall, near to the chancel arch. This was installed in 1748 to commemorate Henry's long life.

Should you thirst for more evidence of his existence, you can visit the Henry Jenkins Inn at Kirkby Malzeard. Henry is depicted, complete with flowing white beard, on the sign outside this hostelry, which stands in the main street of the village. According to local parish records, it has been there for at least 150 years and it replaced the original inn that was situated in Bolton on Swale. Unfortunately, I cannot explain the reason for its transfer to Kirkby Malzeard. Inside the present inn hangs a copy of a genuine portrait of Henry painted by Robert Walker, who was painter to Cromwell. Alongside the portrait are photographs of the monument, church and tablet at Bolton on Swale.

An inexpensive leaflet is available from the inn, which outlines Henry's life and contains the following anecdote regarding the visit to his home by a lawyer searching for evidence in a legal case. As the advocate approached the cottage he saw a feeble, white-haired figure sitting in the front garden. When questioned, this ancient-looking individual said that he knew nothing about the matter and suggested that the visitor entered the cottage and asked his father. The lawyer, mystified, followed his suggestion and inside he found an even older-looking man nodding by the fire. Once again the lawyer was frustrated because this man claimed that his memory was failing, but, his father, who was in the back garden chopping sticks, could tell him all that he needed to know. To his astonishment, the lawyer found Henry in the garden, looking remarkably fit at the age of 166 and far more vigorous than his son and grandson. He was conveniently able to provide the necessary information, which enabled the lawyer to win his case.

If, after reading this account of Henry's remarkable life, you have been galvanised into improving the quality and length of your life and those of your family, the following extracts from *A Collection of 604 Valuable Receipts* may be of assistance. They contain, not only remedies for ailments, but hints on dieting and child care. One word of caution, I cannot vouch for their potency!

A Cold in the Head – Pare very thin the yellow rind of an orange, roll it up inside out and thrust a roll into each nostril.

Bleeding at the Nose – To prevent – Drink much whey every morning and eat a great many raisins.

Gout in the Foot, or Hand – Apply a raw, lean beef-steak, change it every twelve hours till cured.

Indigestion – The best remedy is to eat as much very old Cheshire cheese as you can.

Blisters on the Feet, occasioned by walking – Are cured by drawing a needlefull of worsted through them and leave it till the skin peels off.

Windy Cholic – The best remedy is to eat plentifully of parched peas and also of raw onions.

General Ailments – Cold baths will cure Ague, Apoplexy, Leprosy, Lunacy, The Plague and the bite of a mad dog.

Drowned Persons - Rub the trunk of the body all over with salt. It will recover those that seem dead.

In Extreme Fat – (Dieting) – Use a total vegetable diet, that is, dine on turnips, carrots, or other roots, drinking only water.

Breakfast and sup on milk and water with bread only, for a year.

Children – To Prevent Rickets, Tenderness and Weakness – Dip them in cold water every morning till they are eight or nine months old.

It is best to wean a child when seven months old. It should lie in a cradle at least a year.

Their drink should be water only. Tea they should never taste till ten or twelve years old. Milk, porrage and water gruel are the proper breakfasts for children.

Index